John Paul Stevens and the Constitution

John Paul Stevens
and
the Constitution

The Search for Balance

Robert Judd Sickels

THE PENNSYLVANIA STATE UNIVERSITY PRESS
University Park and London

To Alice, Wendy, Steve, Jane, and Betsy

Library of Congress Cataloging-in-Publication Data

Sickels, Robert J.
John Paul Stevens and the Constitution.

Includes index.
1. Civil rights—United States—Cases. 2. Judicial
review—United States—Cases. 3. Judicial opinions—
United States. 4. Stevens, John Paul, 1920–   .
I. Title.
KF213.S66S56   1988   342.73′085   87–43191
ISBN 0-271-00636-6   347.30285

. . . logic, and history, and custom, and utility, and the accepted standards of right conduct, are the forces which singly or in combination shape the progress of the law. Which of these forces shall dominate in any case must depend largely on the comparative importance or value of the social interests that will be thereby promoted or impaired.

—Benjamin Cardozo

Contents

Preface

This is an analysis of a pragmatic, independent-minded judge's thoughts about judicial review and the Constitution. It is equally a case study of moderation on the Supreme Court and an explanation of one person's cogent variations on that traditional minority theme.

John Paul Stevens's pragmatism takes time to explain in its various applications, as we shall see, though in form it is steady and unwavering throughout his judicial career and must be studied as a coherent whole, for the most part, rather than as an unfolding. His independence is immediately evident, most conveniently in the annual *Harvard Law Review* analysis of Supreme Court voting and opinion-writing: typically he is the most inclined to vote at about the same rate with each of his colleagues, and against each about equally, playing no favorites from left to right. Even among the moderates, he is usually the most independent by this measure. Further, Stevens is one of the most prolific writers of concurring and dissenting opinions: he frequently feels there is something worth saying that no one else has said. It is in these separate opinions, especially, that his substantive contributions and his underlying pragmatism may be found. They are the subject of this book.

A good pragmatist's constitutional theory is inseparable from the legal disputes from which it stems. Stevens's is a theory about deciding individual cases well, not about constitutional principle in the abstract. It follows that the proper way to study his theory of decision making is in its natural factual habitat, in his own words, sometimes at length. Pragmatists on the bench, as elsewhere, deal with ideas retail rather than wholesale: those who would understand them must be concerned about context and study cases.

But there are common themes from case to case, along with differences. In the chapters that follow, the opinions cited and quoted illustrate recurrences, in context. To take familiar points of reference, his approach is broadly reminiscent of Benjamin Cardozo in *The Nature of the Judicial Process* in its eclecticism and practicality and of Alexander Bickel, particularly in *The Least Dangerous Branch,* in its sense of the Supreme Court's place in the social fabric.[1] Stevens is an incrementalist, attuned to the complexity of the Anglo-American legal heritage and yet prepared—and *therefore* prepared—to give the Constitution new meaning as needed, slowly, carefully, and with due respect for the opinions of others. He is *not* the agent of any methodological shortcut or special political doctrine. In many respects he is like Potter Stewart, Byron White, Harry Blackmun, and Lewis Powell, his fellow moderates, using the term loosely, and in some respects not.

I have tried to present Stevens's judicial philosophy evenhandedly, to carve with the grain, respecting facts, giving a thoughtful set of views a full airing and the benefit of an occasional doubt. My purpose in this book is to help explain Stevens to all students of the Court whatever their likes and dislikes. Most who examine his work will have a mixed reaction, as his colleagues have, agreeing with him sometimes, disagreeing sometimes. More to the point, he offers an alternative to the standard liberal and conservative positions and is worth knowing for that alone, whether one thinks him right or wrong on specific issues.

As it happens, in constitutional litigation Stevens is most interested in questions of individual rights. Were this a book about Sandra Day O'Connor, let us say, or William Rehnquist, there would be equal emphasis on the division of power between the national government and the states. But Stevens and the majority of the Court accept the nationalist consensus on the meaning of federalism articulated in *United States v. Carolene Products Co.* and *United States v. Darby Lumber Co.*[2] It is not an area of the law felt to require much exploration or clarification today: it suffices to defer to Congress and to engage in statutory rather than constitutional construction. On questions of economic regulation under the national commerce or taxing and spending powers, accordingly, Stevens can be counted upon neither to dissent (unless the majority jumps the track, as in his judgment it did in its short-lived holding in *National League of Cities v. Usery*) nor to write a separate concurrence (apart from urging his colleagues back on the track in *EEOC v. Wyoming,* reprinted in the Appendix).[3] Similarly, in cases concerning state power to regulate commerce in the absence of federal controls, where decisions turn on facts more than on principle or ideology, Stevens tends to vote quietly with the majority, for the state this time, next time against. In either kind of commerce case, he and the majority seem to feel there is little to dispute. Stevens sharply distinguishes fundamental liberties, which courts must take seriously, and "liberties which derive merely from shifting economic arrangements," which they need not.[4]

Much the same can be said about Stevens and majority consensus in the relatively few cases concerning the separation of national powers. Controversial though they may be in Congress or the country at large, they are fairly easy cases for the Court, decided by large majorities joined by Stevens. Where the issue is presidential versus congressional authority in foreign affairs, the old understanding powerfully affirmed in the *Curtiss-Wright* case in 1936 prevails, in the president's favor.[5] On domestic matters, with no clear rule of deference in operation, the Court decides on the merits of the case at hand. The rulings on the unconstitutionality of the legislative veto and the Gramm-Rudman-Hollings budget-balancing act are cases in point.[6]

There are statutory matters on which Stevens has made his mark—notably antitrust, in private practice, in the fifties as associate counsel of a House subcommittee studying monopoly power and member of the National Committee to Study Anti-Trust Laws, and later as circuit judge. His early interest in contextual facts and the competitive effects of business activities rather than abstractions and formulas is at one with his antitrust decisions on the Supreme Court[7] and his pragmatism in general. But at the level of constitutional interpretation the attention of the Court, and of Justice Stevens even more acutely, is on freedom of expression and religion, due process, and equal protection of the laws. This book follows his lead.

1

Judicial Pragmatism

John Paul Stevens has been something of an enigma since his appointment to the Supreme Court in 1975. As the only new arrival in the years between 1972 and 1981, he was understandably the focus of attention and, specifically, of speculation whether a divided Court would now tip right or left. But it was unclear what kind of justice he would be. The reports of his background offered mixed clues: a Republican, son of a prominent Republican businessman in Chicago, named by Republican presidents to the federal court of appeals and then to the Supreme Court, yet in 1947 and 1948 clerk to a Democrat, Wiley Rutledge, one of the most liberal justices ever to sit on the Court, of whose work Stevens had written admiringly in later years. Stevens's opinions as a circuit judge and later as Supreme Court justice put him in no familiar ideological camp. A "maverick," a "gadfly," a "wild card," an intrigued press said, "free of preconceived notions," the Court's "least predictable member."[1] As it turned out he did not move the Court one way or the other, though in recent years particularly he has edged to the liberal side.

Today there is still no widespread understanding of Justice Stevens's judicial philosophy. Yet solid evidence of consistency in his approach to the law and judging is to be found in his opinions. Because it is the consistency of pragmatic method and concern for clarity, rather than of conservatism or liberalism, it has not caught the public eye.

Stevens came to the federal bench with a judicial role well formed in his mind, and he has kept to it since. I begin with his earliest opinions, not to provide a footing for contrasting his later work, but ultimately to demonstrate that what is characteristic of his judging today was characteristic from the outset. His first published opinion as a circuit judge was a strong defense of individual liberty. Dissenting, he argued that the Wisconsin Assembly had denied Father James Groppi due process of law in violation of the Fourteenth Amendment: it had improperly convicted him of disorderly conduct for staging an occupation of the assembly chamber and preventing the legislature from doing its business. Father Groppi had led a group of protesters into the chamber and up to the speaker's stand, declared his intention to remain until the legislators restored funds cut from the welfare budget, and in fact held out from noon till midnight. Two days later, in his absence, the Assembly found Father Groppi in contempt and sentenced him to jail for the remainder of the legislative session. Judge Stevens, on appeal, had no quarrel with the substance of the decision as affirmed by fellow members of the court of appeals. No one, he said, could contend that Father Groppi's case had been brought to an unfair or unreasonable conclusion. He had unquestionably disrupted the legislature. He never contended that he was innocent or the sentence excessive.[2]

What Judge Stevens did find wrong, however, was the denial of Father Groppi's procedural rights, foremost among them the right to a hearing. "One of the oldest and most consistently accepted maxims in our legal tradition," he said, "is the proposition that 'no man shall be punished before he has had an opportunity of being heard.'" Wisconsin should have allowed Father Groppi a hearing before the Assembly or, better yet, provided for the prosecution of contempts in a court of law with full procedural safeguards, as had other states. Judges, he said, can be trusted. In defense of hewing to traditional procedures, he cited Oliver Wendell Holmes, Jr., and Louis Brandeis, among others,[3] four centuries of Anglo-American legal tradition, and certain practical concerns:

> It is argued that there was no risk of error or abuse in this case because petitioner's disorderly conduct occurred "in the immediate view of" the Wisconsin Assembly. It is contended that no purpose could have been served by hearing from petitioner or his counsel because the Assembly

already knew all the facts. This may or may not be true. It is entirely possible that conduct which certain legislators found particularly offensive was committed by other members of the "gathering of people" led by the petitioner; it is possible that some legislators were particularly offended by insulting speech (perhaps even speech on other occasions) rather than conduct; and that certain conduct was viewed by some legislators but not by others. Even if each member of the Assembly who voted in favor of the resolution had perfect knowledge of the facts, a valid purpose would have been served by hearing from petitioner before voting on the resolution. It is presumed that argument may persuade judges even when they know the facts. I would give legislators the benefit of the same presumption.[4]

Reading the *Groppi* opinion alone, one might suppose Stevens to be a libertarian, a defender of unpopular causes, a judicial activist confident of the authority of judges and legal tradition to correct the indiscretions of elected officials. But the supposition would be wide of the mark. As seen in his very next due process opinion, also a dissent, the *Groppi* case revealed only one facet of Judge Stevens's thinking about law and justice.

One William C. Smith had pleaded guilty to charges of drug dealing, having been informed of the maximum sentence he might receive on each count, though not of his statutory ineligibility for parole. Months later he sought reversal of his conviction and sentence. Failing in district court, he persuaded a majority of the court of appeals that he had been unfairly treated. Judge Stevens dissented. Ineligibility for parole, he said, was one piece of information, along with the expected sentence, that an accused might well wish to have before plea bargaining. But the failure of the trial judge to mention the ineligibility did not render a guilty plea involuntary, nor was acceptance of the plea fundamentally unfair.[5]

The *Groppi* dissent appears liberal and principled, the *Smith* dissent cautious and deferential. On the surface there is little to suggest the hand of one man. Judge Stevens proves to be a dissenter of some force in both cases, it is true. "Since I find myself out of step not only with respected colleagues but also with a whole parade of recent decisions," he says in the latter, "I shall explain at some length why I am convinced the parade is march-

ing in the wrong direction."[6] But there the similarity seems to
end. His is the only voice for Groppi, the only one against Smith.
And there are differences in approach. In *Groppi* he restates a
simple rule from which it follows logically that due process was
denied in the case at hand; in *Smith* he rejects a simple rule:

> Fundamental fairness may require discussion of certain
> important consequences in specific cases, but a rigid rule
> that makes a guilty plea vulnerable whenever a trial judge
> fails to supplement counsel's advice with an enumeration
> of all significant consequences of the plea is neither neces-
> sary to the maintenance of civilized standards of procedure
> nor desirable.[7]

There should be no fixed formula either way. The goal should be
to decide each case on its merits. In some circumstances the
judge's silence would be shockingly unfair; in this case it was not.[8]

In the *Smith* opinion Stevens also shows concern about the consequences of his decisions. Most criminal convictions stem from
guilty pleas, he notes, to which a busy judiciary should not invite
unnecessary challenge.

> The reasons for narrowly limiting the grounds for collat-
> eral attack on final judgments are well known and basic to
> our adversary system of justice. Every inroad on the con-
> cept of finality undermines confidence in the integrity of
> our procedures; and, by increasing the volume of judicial
> work, inevitably delays and impairs the orderly adminis-
> tration of justice.
> . . . I fear that the premises on which the decision rests
> will significantly increase the required colloquy between
> the accused and the court, and thereby multiply the possi-
> bilities of error, occupy valuable court time, and rarely be
> productive except when the accused is not represented by
> counsel.[9]

Further, contrasted with such costs, the benefits are insubstantial, since most such challenges in no way raise the likelihood of
discovery that an innocent person has been convicted. It is better
on balance to give most responsibility for advising defendants to
counsel and leave trial judges free to judge.[10]

While in *Groppi* Judge Stevens is not at all deferential to the initial decision maker, the Wisconsin Assembly, in *Smith* he argues for a large measure of deference to the federal district judge who accepted a plea of guilty—and to counsel, in his view the prime guarantor of justice in a criminal trial.

> . . . I am concerned that the rule of this case tends to place a greater premium on a required ritual than on the fair exercise of judgment by experienced trial judges and trial lawyers. In my opinion, both due process in the constitutional sense and the practical administration of the day to day business of the courts will be better served by placing greater confidence in the trial bench and the bar.

A close examination of the record, including the exchanges of judge, defendant, and counsel, leads him to the conclusion that injustice was not done.[11]

For all their apparent dissimilarity, however, the *Groppi* and *Smith* dissents are substantially consistent with one another. Both show faith in trial courts and concern for clear principle and full facts as necessary ingredients of good decisions. In *Groppi* the legislature ignored an old and important principle regarding the opportunity to be heard and thereby foreclosed the fact-finding that would be routine in a court; in *Smith* an appellate court experimented with a questionable new rule, and in so doing overlooked indications in the factual record developed by the trial court and reviewed in all its detail on appeal that Smith had not been ill-treated. It is a constant theme in Stevens's judicial opinions: the best decisions are likely to be made by trial judges equipped with well-crafted rules (including constitutional principles, statutes, and precedent) and the discretion to fit them intelligently to the facts of each case and to the wider needs of the legal system. Appellate courts (and legislatures) should not try to stand in their place.

Rules

Stevens values clarity in the legal process with the same intensity some justices value liberal or conservative results. As a judge, he is most comfortable guided by a law with reasonably clear and settled meaning in its own terms and in its legislative and judicial history. In applying the law, he willingly makes use of judicial constructions that both serve the ends of the law in question and make its meaning clear and accessible. In his *Groppi* dissent, for example, he applies a judge-made elaboration of the Due Process Clause of the Fourteenth Amendment (that "no man shall be punished before he has had an opportunity of being heard") with vigor and conviction. Another judge might be less confident, if only because due process has been so differently understood from generation to generation. But to Stevens the concept of due process has a rich coherence. He quotes Felix Frankfurter:

> "Expressing as it does in its ultimate analysis respect enforced by law for that feeling of just treatment which has been evolved through centuries of Anglo-American constitutional history and civilization, 'due process' cannot be imprisoned within the treacherous limits of any formula. Representing a profound attitude of fairness between man and man, and more particularly between the individual and government, 'due process' is compounded of history, reason, the past course of decisions, and stout confidence in the strength of the democratic faith which we profess."[12]

The clause gives clear direction, as does its time-honored component, the requirement of a hearing. The conclusion follows: it is an issue of the greatest importance; adherence to established and respected procedures requires that the legislative contempt without hearing be set aside.[13]

On the other hand, he opposes judge-made formulas that oversimplify in a search for "delusive exactness" (Stevens quoting Holmes),[14] ignoring points of law and fact that would contribute to a better judgment. His criticism of "required ritual" in *Smith* is an example.[15] Stevens's objection to such formulas is not that of the rule skeptics, that logically they cannot work, but that they blind the judge to relevant information that might lead to wiser decisions. Wiley Rutledge, he writes, "exhibited great respect for experience and practical considerations. He was critical of broadly phrased rules which deceptively suggested that they would simplify the decision of difficult questions."[16] A good illustration of this point is his opinion for the circuit court in a case involving a dress code for public-school teachers in Illinois.

> If a school board should correctly conclude that a teacher's style of dress or plumage has an adverse impact on the educational process, and if that conclusion conflicts with the teacher's interest in selecting his own lifestyle, we have no doubt that the interest of the teacher is subordinate to the public interest. We must assume, however, that sometimes such a school board determination will be incorrect. Even on that assumption, we are persuaded that the importance of allowing school boards sufficient latitude to discharge their responsibilities effectively—and inevitably, therefore, to make mistakes from time to time—outweighs the individual interest at stake. We do not imply that diversity and individualism among members of the teaching profession is less desirable than conformity; the critical point is that each choice between conformity and diversity is itself affected by a variety of factors, and local school boards need the freedom to make diverse choices for themselves.
>
> If such choices must be tested against a federal constitutional standard, perhaps Vandyke beards and three button suits—or possibly shaven heads and t-shirts—will be permissible for all teachers throughout the nation. In the name of maximizing the individual teacher's freedom to appear as he pleases, such a constitutional rule would minimize the areas of choice available to local school boards in determining the impact of teacher appearance on the educational process, and on the associational interests of the children for whose education they are responsible.[17]

A national rule about Vandyke beards would work in the limited sense that it could be reasonably well understood and enforced. But to prohibit only one beard style, or a few, would be arbitrary even if there were no objection to beard regulations as such. Judges need "principled standards," not "mere labels or formulae."[18]

Stevens also opposes unduly complex judge-made rules. In taking more and more values into consideration in the administration of a legal rule, sometimes also striving for clarity and evenhanded enforcement, courts at times add refinement upon refinement to the basic statement and, he argues, in the end only make the rule less clear, its application less certain. He describes the problems in his opinion of the Court in *United States v. Ross* in 1982, upholding the heroin conviction of Albert "Bandit" Ross, whose car, including a paper bag and a zippered leather pouch in the trunk, had been searched for drugs after a lawful arrest. The rules of search and seizure were so complex at the time that the district court could approve the search of the bag and the pouch, containing heroin and cash, respectively, a panel of the court of appeals the search of the pouch but not the bag, and the court of appeals en banc, on rehearing, neither.[19] Stripping away accretions of precedent involving questions of the relative expectation of privacy one might have with respect to different kinds of containers, Stevens enunciates a rule that allows a complete search, defined only by the object of the search and the place in which there is probable cause to believe it will be found: "We hold that they may conduct a search of the vehicle that is as thorough as a magistrate could authorize in a warrant 'particularly describing the place to be searched.'"[20] It is a return to the simplicity of *Carroll v. United States* (1925), the Supreme Court's original automobile-search decision.[21] Stevens's opinion bristles with statements about the importance of clarifying the law,[22] supported by pragmatic arguments for a simple, understandable search and seizure rule.[23] As we shall see, he advances comparable arguments in separate opinions in cases on obscenity, the establishment of religion, and the equal protection of the law.

Stevens reasons cleanly and would have the Court do the same, with rules as unadorned as the facts and exigencies of life permit.

Facts

"[N]o general statement can really be understood until it has acquired meaning through case by case application," wrote Stevens in 1974, in the spirit of William James. "Pragmatism is uncomfortable away from facts," said James. "The pragmatist clings to facts and concreteness, observes truth at its work in particular cases, and generalizes. Truth, for him, becomes a class-name for all sorts of definite working-values in experience." In James's terms, Stevens is a "tough-minded" empiricist—fact-hungry, pluralistic, and skeptical—not "tender-minded," dogmatic rationalist.[24] He twits his more tender-minded colleagues for their easy generalizations. When the majority found reason for prison shakedown searches and other harsh practices in the violent nature of prison populations, citing aggregate prison-murder figures, Stevens parried with statistics indicating that the homicide rate was actually greater in the general population in a number of American metropolitan areas. He added:

> The Court's portrayal of the stereotypical prison inmate entirely overlooks the wide range of individuals who have actually served and do serve time in the prison system. It ignores, for example, the conscientious objectors who refuse to register for the draft, and the corporate executives who have been convicted of violating securities, antitrust, or tax laws, union leaders, former White House aides, former Governors, judges, and legislators, famous writers and sports heroes, and many thousands who have committed serious offenses but for whom crime is by no means a way of life.[25]

The importance of facts for Stevens in both trial and appellate proceedings, and of the need to avoid abstract and simplistic solutions, is seen in his criticism of summary judgments. A case may be decided summarily without full presentation of arguments and facts if the court deems the information at hand sufficient. To the pragmatist, it is a procedure that dramatically increases the likelihood of error.

Justice Stevens criticized the Supreme Court's procedures, and its logic, when it summarily decided that Frank Snepp, formerly of the Central Intelligence Agency, would have to give the government all past and future income from *Decent Interval* because in writing the book he had violated his agreement not to release official information without agency approval. The Court was imposing a drastic and unprecedented sanction unauthorized by law, even though, as it conceded, the book contained not a word of classified material and thus did not compromise the government's interest in secrecy for which the agreement with Snepp had been concluded.[26]

The uninhibited character of today's exercise in lawmaking is highlighted by the Court's disregard of two venerable principles that favor a more conservative approach to this case.

First, for centuries the English-speaking judiciary refused to grant equitable relief unless the plaintiff could show that his remedy at law was inadequate. Without waiting for an opportunity to appraise the adequacy of the punitive damages remedy in this case, the Court has jumped to the conclusion that equitable relief is necessary.

Second, and of greater importance, the Court seems unaware of the fact that its drastic new remedy has been fashioned to enforce a species of prior restraint on a citizen's right to criticize his government. Inherent in this prior restraint is the risk that the reviewing agency will misuse its authority to delay the publication of a critical work or to persuade an author to modify the contents of his work beyond the demands of secrecy. The character of the covenant as a prior restraint on free speech surely imposes an especially heavy burden on the censor to justify the remedy it seeks. It would take more than the Court has written to persuade me that the burden has been met.[27]

Similarly, in *Pennsylvania v. Mimms* it was inadequacy of fact, and of law, that led Justice Stevens to dissent from the Court's summary judgment. The central question was whether, under the Fourth and Fourteenth Amendments, a police officer might order a person lawfully detained for driving without a current license plate to step out of his car. It is crucial, he says, that the Court have the benefit of differing judicial assessments before an issue is decided for once and for all. In this case the Court, in haste, has fashioned a wholly new rule based on some quick guesses about police safety.[28]

Stevens concludes that the Court has its facts wrong, having misread the literature it cites on the relative danger of ordering and not ordering people from their cars. Reviewing questions that might be raised in a less hurried proceeding, he adds that "we should give further consideration to the infinite variety of situations in which today's holding may be applied."

The Court cannot seriously believe that the risk to the arresting officer is so universal that his safety is *always* a reasonable justification for ordering a driver out of his car. The commuter on his way home to dinner, the parent driving children to school, the tourist circling the Capitol, or the family on a Sunday afternoon outing hardly pose the same threat as a driver curbed after a high-speed chase through a high-crime area late at night. Nor is it universally true that the driver's interest in remaining in the car is negligible. A woman stopped at night may fear for her own safety; a person in poor health may object to standing in the cold or rain; another who left home in haste to drive children or spouse to school or to the train may not be fully dressed; an elderly driver who presents no possible threat of violence may regard the police command as nothing more than an arrogant and unnecessary display of authority.[29]

Summary judgments, then, are suspect to a pragmatist such as Stevens and provide an occasion for dissenting statements on the uses of factual inquiry. Much the same can be said of premature "advisory" opinions: to accept a question of law before it is played out in a specific controversy is to approach the interpretation of words hypothetically, out of context. He mentions the special need to decide cases on concrete facts in one such case. In another he says, "When we follow our traditional practice of adjudicating difficult and novel constitutional questions only in concrete factual situations, the adjudications tend to be crafted with greater wisdom. Hypothetical rulings are inherently treacherous and prone to lead us into unforeseen errors; they are qualitatively less reliable than the products of case-by-case adjudication."[30] A case without fact, whatever the reason, is to be avoided.

Even in that overwhelming majority of cases in which there is an adequate record and full argument before the Court, however, a good pragmatist's approach is distinctive. In these cases, too, Stevens stresses the importance of facts—even to the point, as he puts it, of letting the facts speak for themselves.

In a few instances the facts simply overwhelm the principles that would normally apply. The most striking example is *Nixon v. Administrator of General Services*. In 1974 a distrustful Congress deprived Richard Nixon, alone among American presidents, of the custody of his presidential tapes and papers, abrogating an agreement he had made with the General Services Administration affording him a veto over all public or private use of such materials. The act, signed by President Ford, gave custody of the materials to the GSA and provided for government archivists to screen out personal items to be returned to the former president and for eventual public access to some of the remainder.

The Supreme Court, in an opinion by Justice Brennan, upheld the legislation, responding to each of several constitutional complaints, among them that, in singling out Richard Nixon for punitive treatment, Congress had passed a bill of attainder in violation of Article I of the Constitution. The Court decided that the act was not punitive, but was instead a reasonable attempt to see that presidential papers and tapes were properly preserved. Given the risks created by the Nixon-GSA agreement, Nixon could be regarded as "a legitimate class of one."[31]

Concurring, Justice Stevens agreed there was a class of one, but took judicial notice of two facts the Court had not mentioned: Nixon's resignation "under unique circumstances" and his acceptance of a pardon for any offenses committed during his presidency. By these actions he had set himself apart. In the absence of such extraordinary facts in the record, however, a court could not properly allow Congress to treat a single unpopular president harshly.[32] Perhaps for the Court the resignation and pardon are implicit in its judgment that the facts of the case are unique. For Stevens they are the necessary, explicit reasons why the act is not a bill of attainder.

Another case, factually very different, allowed Stevens to make the same kind of point. It was an air quality decision in 1978, from which he dissented on the ground that the unique characteristics of asbestos as a pollutant justify a unique regulation. The Environmental Protection Agency required the wetting down of asbestos insulation in buildings undergoing demolition. The legalistic conclusion of the Court is that under the terms of the Clean Air Act such a rule is a mere "work practice standard," rather than an "emission standard" backed by stringent criminal sanctions. Stevens reviews the facts at length (of the four opinions, his is the only one to explain the dangers of asbestos) and concludes that, although the wetting standard is not quantitative like other emission standards, it is legally equivalent. It is not expressed numerically because asbestos pollution is not measurable numerically. Since asbestos is one of three toxic substances the pertinent provision of the act specifically requires the EPA to regulate, he says, the Court "should avoid a construction of the statute that would deny the Administrator the authority to regulate these poisonous substances effectively."[33]

A comparable use of unusual facts can be seen in a circuit court case questioning the legality of a congressman's conduct in mailing certain questionnaires at public expense. Were the questionnaires official business qualifying for franking or "private" communications to advance the congressman's candidacy for re-election? It is a question of intent. Stevens rejects two fact-finding approaches. One, suggested by the plaintiff, a candidate opposing the congressman in the forthcoming election, would deny free postage to any congressional mailing motivated by a desire to please the electorate. Too broad, says Stevens: such a desire is neither unexpected nor inappropriate in an elected official. Another, from the defendant, to the effect that motive is irrelevant and that content alone should be judged, is also rejected, because of the ease with which private purpose might be clothed in language of the common good. Instead, Stevens suggests better, "extrinsic," evidence of intent: the crucial facts, he says, are that the congressman was running for re-election in an entirely new district and that the bulk of the questionnaires were sent there rather than to present constituents. There is no rule that a member of Congress must send mail only within the district he represents, but the fact that a large mailing of questionnaires, the first in his four terms in office, prominently featuring his name and face, was directed to prospective voters who were not then his constituents made it clear to Judge Stevens that the member's purpose was the private one of promoting his own candidacy.[34]

These are facts that hit a judge squarely in the face. They are also the kind that seldom turn up in court. The judge who waits for diagnostic facts of such clarity before reversing an official decision—in this case of a single member of Congress—is exercising a good measure of judicial restraint. The tendency is the same at any level of generality, applying the Constitution to a statute (the *Nixon* case), a statute to a regulation (the asbestos case), or statutes and regulations to specific disputes (as in the franking case). It is an approach we shall note particularly in Stevens's opinions on racial discrimination in Chapter 4.

(At the other extreme, of course, there are facts, however interesting, that must not be allowed to influence an appellate court's judgment. Thus in a case involving the denial of counsel, Justice Stevens, characteristically wary of irrelevancies, writes a concur-

rence to counter the emotionalism of the dissenting opinions of
Warren Burger and Harry Blackmun, who make much of the
"savage murder of a small child" and the "brutal, tragic, and hei-
nous crime." The crime as such is only a "surface issue," in Stevens's view. The emotional aspects of the case are a challenge, he
concludes, but the Court has an obligation to confine its attention
to facts bearing on the issues under review.)[35]

Balancing

Most appellate cases cannot fairly be settled by the force of a few
striking facts. Typically, instead, there is a quantity of evidence
and argument on each side and a need to weigh one against the
other. The pragmatist's role in ordinary cases is to press for full
information, then to balance.

A good illustration is Stevens's concurrence in *H & H Tire Co.
v. United States Department of Transportation,* a case of statutory
interpretation before the court of appeals in 1972. At issue was
the legality of a safety standard of the National Highway Traffic
Safety Administration requiring that certain laboratory performance tests for new automobile tires also be applied to retreaded
tires. H & H Tire Co., a retreader, alleged that the standard was
impracticable, unreasonable, and fashioned in violation of procedures required by law. The court found that the agency had presented too little evidence in favor of such tests and too little about
the costs to retreaders and the motoring public. "[P]urchasers of
retreads are often persons who cannot afford new tires or who,
because of the expense of new tires, continue to use worn out tires
much longer than they, in safety, should."[36]

Judge Stevens concurred, but sketched the fact-gathering requirement of the law far more broadly. A proper cost-benefit analysis encompasses the availability of alternative, less costly regulations—even the likely effect of retread standards on the price
of new tires. He illustrates:

> As they are used, tires become less safe. Anyone who
> elects to drive at an excessive speed or on tires that have
> already traveled thousands of miles over a variety of road

surfaces assumes some risk of tire failure. For that reason, at some point in time most car owners make a choice among four alternatives: (1) to continue driving on the old tires they own; (2) to replace them with somewhat better used tires; (3) to replace them with retreads; or (4) to replace them with new tires.

Respondent has determined that the third alternative may not be selected unless the retread will last as long and perform just as well as a new tire. If that determination is enforced, the cost of retreads will increase and inevitably some car owners will reject the third alternative. Some will prolong their use of old tires; some will replace worn tires with others that are only slightly better; and the most cautious will pay the price of a new set of tires which may have a longer life expectancy than the used vehicle on which they will be placed. Thus, among the predictable effects of the enforcement of Standard 117 are the following: (1) some people will be driving on less safe tires; (2) some people will buy more expensive tires than they really need; and (3) since fewer retreads will be sold, new tire manufacturers will have less vigorous competition to face. In short, there is a cost to society at large associated with the enforcement of Standard 117.

On the other hand, it is no doubt true that the sale of defective retreads, or the sale of retreads that will not perform as long or as well as drivers anticipate, may pose a significant safety hazard. My problem with this case stems from the fact that there is nothing in the record to indicate that respondent assessed the magnitude of that potential hazard, or considered whether measures specifically mentioned in the statute, such as fair labeling, tire quality grading, and limits on the age of tire carcasses which can be retreaded, would sufficiently protect the consumer without curtailing his choice among apparently acceptable alternatives.[37]

In this instance the agency failed to do its job.

Variations on the fact-gathering-and-balancing theme are seen in judgments about the conduct of a trial ("the trial itself, viewed as an entirety, was not fundamentally unfair") and in the assignment of variable rather than fixed weight to constitutional values ("due process is a flexible concept which takes account of the importance of the interests at stake").[38] An illustration of the latter is afforded by the *Miller* dress-code case, noted above.

In *Miller,* Stevens reviews precedent asserting and precedent denying that hairstyle and dress are included in the "liberty" protected by the guarantee of due process. His own position, with which he concludes, is that hairstyle and dress indeed are protected, but not much, all things considered. They may express a religious or political conviction, a national or family heritage, or aid in the projection of a personal image, any of which may reasonably be construed as an aspect of liberty under the Constitution.[39] But if one's choice of appearance is a constitutionally protected interest in liberty, it is a relatively minor one and under some circumstances may be overridden.[40]

> From the earliest days of organized society, no absolute right to an unfettered choice of appearance has ever been recognized; matters of appearance and dress have always been subjected to control and regulation, sometimes by custom and social pressure, sometimes by legal rules. A variety of reasons justify limitations on this interest. They include a concern for public health or safety, a desire to avoid specific forms of antisocial conduct, and an interest in protecting the beholder from unsightly displays. Nothing more than a desire to encourage respect for tradition, or for those who are moved by traditional ceremonies, may be sufficient in some situations. Indeed, even an interest in teaching respect for (though not necessarily agreement with) traditional manners, may lend support to some public grooming requirements. Therefore, just as the individual has an interest in a choice among different styles of appearance and behavior, and a democratic society has an interest in fostering diverse choices, so also does society have a legitimate interest in placing limits on the exercise of that choice.[41]

To summarize, the thrust of Stevens's decisions is that good appellate judgments depend heavily on facts, and that on occasion one or a few facts are decisive, but that far more often it is necessary to perform a cost-benefit analysis of a larger number. His trust is in rules and facts together rather than mere abstract principles of law. Thus in his nomination hearing he responded to a question of legal principle with a statement of the "burden of factual presentation to enable a factfinder to know that this is not merely a formula of words,"[42] and in an essay on Wiley Rutledge, Stevens wrote:

> Quite clearly, the principal explanation for the length of his opinions has nothing to do with his style. Instead, the length was primarily a matter of finding it necessary to say a great deal in order to explain fully the reasons for his decisions. If the case turned on its facts, all material facts were carefully reviewed. Whether facts or law were controlling, the argument to be met was fully stated in order to make the precise import of the decision clear. When policy considerations, such as the need to combat inflation in the midst of war, seemed overwhelmingly to demand a result which Rutledge could not accept, he candidly acknowledged the force of those considerations before outlining the reasons which he found more compelling. To me, Rutledge's long opinions are evidence of two virtues of a great judge—tolerance and judgment. The full statement of the opposing argument and countervailing considerations reflects a habit of understanding before disagreeing. The full statement of all the factors which lead to and qualify the result which is eventually reached—though exasperating to a hurried practitioner seeking a succinct statement of a "true rule"—indicates that the faculty of judgment and not merely the logical application of unbending principles has been employed to resolve an actual controversy between litigants.[43]

Consequences

A closely related element of Stevens's legal philosophy is his concern for the consequences of judicial decisions: it is, as James said, "the attitude of looking away from first things, principles, 'categories,' supposed necessities; and of looking towards last things, fruits, consequences, facts."[44] The consequences upon which he

focuses may be for the parties to the case at hand, for those who
will be less directly affected by today's decision as tomorrow's
precedent, or, more typically, both together; and they may be for
litigants, the courts, other parts of the government, or the public
at large. (In the *Smith* case, as we have already noted, Stevens is
concerned about attacks on guilty pleas in part because of unset-
tling effects on judicial workloads, the orderly administration of
justice, and public confidence in the judiciary.)[45] A sampling of
other cases reveals the diversity of his concern.

Stevens's interest in the specific effects of judges' decisions (and
similarly of pretrial events) can be seen in his common-sense assessment of the reactions of jurors and suspects to what is said
and done in their presence. In one of his first cases he cautioned
that a defendant's decision not to testify would in all likelihood
be prejudicial, despite the efforts of the judge or counsel. In 1978
he dissented from the Court's holding that a judge, against the
wishes of a defendant, might comment on the latter's refusal to
testify on his own behalf. The trial judge's comment was not, to
be sure, that the jury might draw adverse conclusions from the
defendant's silence, but that it might *not*. Even so, the defendant
felt the unintended effect would be to call attention to his failure
to testify. Stevens agreed.[46]

The next year, Stevens argued in dissent that it was unlikely
that jurors would obey a trial judge's order to ignore a codefen-
dant's confession, citing Learned Hand ("the recommendation to
the jury of a mental gymnastic which is beyond, not only their
powers, but anybody else's") and Robert Jackson ("The naive assumption that prejudicial effects can be overcome by instructions
to the jury, all practicing lawyers know to be unmitigated fic-
tion").[47]

In an analogous case, *Rhode Island v. Innis,* Stevens concluded
that the likely (and intended) effect of a policeman's remarks in
the presence of a suspect was greater than the majority of the
Court presumed. Innis was picked up by the police in the vicinity
of an armed robbery, read his rights, and placed in a car for the
ride to the police station after stating a desire to see an attorney.
An officer ordered to ride in the back with Innis said en route that
there was a school for handicapped children nearby and "God
forbid" that one of the children should find the shotgun used in
the robbery and be hurt. Innis forthwith told the police where the
shotgun could be found.[48] Was the remark permissible, as the

Court held, or was it "interrogation" within the meaning of *Miranda v. Arizona?* Says Stevens, if the definition of "interrogation" is to be meaningful, it must cover police statements or actions that have the *effect* of questioning. A suspect's rights are jeopardized by any attempts to obtain information after a suspect has decided not to be questioned.[49]

> In any event, I think the Court is clearly wrong in holding, as a matter of law, that Officer Gleckman should not have realized that his statement was likely to elicit an incriminating response. The Court implicitly assumes that, at least in the absence of a lengthy harangue, a criminal suspect will not be likely to respond to indirect appeals to his humanitarian impulses. . . .
> The Court's assumption . . . is directly contrary to the teachings of police interrogation manuals, which recommend appealing to a suspect's sense of morality as a standard and often successful interrogation technique.[50]

From a popular criminal interrogation manual, Stevens cites a section titled "Urge the Subject to Tell the Truth for the Sake of His Own Conscience, Mental Relief, or Moral Well-being, as Well as 'for the Sake of Everybody Concerned,' and Also Because It Is 'the Only Decent and Honorable Thing to Do.'"[51] There is, in short, reason to suspect that Innis was undergoing deliberate interrogation.

In another case, *In re Chase,* he dissented on pragmatic grounds from the judgment of the court of appeals that a criminal defendant might be punished for repeated failure to rise when the judge entered the courtroom. Stevens assumed that spectators, counsel, and court personnel might be forced to rise to mark the beginning and ending of sessions or, more to the point, "because the tradition emphasizes the solemnity and majesty of the judicial process and thus increases the probability that witnesses will speak the truth and advocacy will be rational and not just emotional."[52] But the defendant, not in the room by choice, should not be required to rise in respect, since his conscience might dictate otherwise.[53] Since failure to rise might well prejudice a jury, there is no need for a judge to add deterrents of his own for the future. We may count on counsel to tell the defendant, as Chase was told, of the practical wisdom of standing up, Stevens says. It is a problem unlikely to recur.[54] Stevens's assessment of the danger to the judicial system contrasts with that of the trial judge, who imposed consecutive sentences of three days for each failure to rise—a total of 297 days in prison, to be served in addition to the five-year term for conviction on charges related to the destruction of draft-board records.

Such opinions analyze the impact of words and events in a given situation. In every case, however, as *Chase* illustrates, Stevens is also concerned about the subsequent use of decisions as precedent, a concern that is clearest when he votes to refuse a case for want of generality.[55] As a pragmatist he prefers that holdings be not only correct but effective, killing a number of present and future birds with one stone (of course without violating the pragmatist's contrary rule against overgeneralization). He is cool toward issues he thinks are both isolated and trivial: "We are far too busy to correct every error that we perceive among the thousands of cases that litigants ask us to review. . . . Today we exercise our majestic power to enforce a School Board's suspension of a 10th-grade student who consumed too much alcohol on October 21, 1980," he says derisively. "If the student had been unjustly suspended, I wonder if the Court would consider the matter of sufficient national importance to require summary reversal. I doubt it."[56] He quotes Chief Justice Vinson: "To remain effective, the Supreme Court must continue to decide only those cases which present questions whose resolution will have immediate importance far beyond the particular facts and parties involved."[57] The cases involving jury instructions and police officers' tendentious remarks qualify.

In one case, *Kissinger v. Reporters Committee,* Stevens's *sole* concern is for the implications of the case as precedent. Objecting to the Court's decision allowing certain notes taken from the Department of State to be kept confidential by the former secretary, he saw no reason for concern about the result in the case at hand, but worried that the decision might create an incentive for others to counter the Freedom of Information Act by taking potentially embarrassing files home.[58] In other cases, however, taking the long view has costs for Stevens: he sometimes follows precedent for the systemic benefits of continuity in the law, even though the precedent is flawed. "Judges, more than most, should understand the value of adherence to settled procedures. By adopting a set of fair procedures, and then adhering to them, courts of law ensure that justice is administered with an even hand."[59] In one instance, for example, finding the controlling precedent wrong, although not egregiously so, he wrote:

> Of even greater importance, however, is my concern about the potential damage to the legal system that may be caused by frequent or sudden reversals of direction that may appear to have been occasioned by nothing more significant than a change in the identity of this Court's personnel. Granting that a zigzag is sometimes the best course [citing the flag-salute cases], I am firmly convinced that we have a profound obligation to give recently decided cases the strongest presumption of validity. That presumption is supported by much more than the desire to foster an appearance of certainty and impartiality in the administration of justice, or the interest in facilitating the labors of judges. The presumption is an essential thread in the mantle of protection that the law affords the individual. Citizens must have confidence that the rules on which they rely in ordering their affairs—particularly when they are prepared to take issue with those in power in doing so—are rules of law and not merely the opinions of a small group of men who temporarily occupy high office. It is the unpopular or beleaguered individual—not the man in power—who has the greatest stake in the integrity of the law.
>
> For me, the adverse consequences of adhering to an arguably erroneous precedent in this case are far less serious than the consequences of further unravelling the doctrine of *stare decisis*. I therefore join the Court's disposition.[60]

In another case he followed precedent that in his judgment defied the intent of Congress, in part because he found it in tune with the times, therefore workable:

> Mr. Justice Cardozo noted: "[W]hen a rule, after it has been duly tested by experience, has been found to be inconsistent with the sense of justice or with the social welfare, there should be less hesitation in frank avowal and full abandonment. . . . If judges have woefully misinterpreted the *mores* of their day, or if the *mores* of their day are no longer those of ours, they ought not to tie, in helpless submission, the hands of their successors." In this case, those

admonitions favor adherence to, rather than departure from, precedent. For even if *Jones* did not accurately reflect the sentiments of the Reconstruction Congress, it surely accords with the prevailing sense of justice today.[61]

In 1987 Stevens abandoned his objections to benign discrimination, accepting the majority view that the Civil Rights Act of 1984 allows the preferential treatment of women and minorities. Though the legislative history remains unambiguous, the majority position has become "an important part of the fabric of our law" and merits observance for the "stability and orderly development of the law." His tolerance is not unlimited, however. With regard to one states'-rights opinion of Justice Rehnquist he said, "I think it so plain that *National League of Cities* not only was incorrectly decided, but also is inconsistent with the central purpose of the Constitution itself, that it is not entitled to the deference that the doctrine of *stare decisis* ordinarily commands for the Court's precedents."[62]

Stevens's concern for consequences does not mean that statutory and constitutional mandates should be ignored in the pursuit of one's own policy preferences. (In an opinion for the court of appeals, for example, he refused to extend the constitutional right to counsel to a parole hearing, sensible though it might seem to do so, because the issue as he saw it was whether the hearing was covered by the Sixth Amendment, not whether it was important.)[63] It does mean that, within the bounds of proper discretion, workable results should be sought.

More generally, as he notes in another case, *stare decisis* provides "busy judges with a valid reason for refusing to remeasure a delicate balance that has tipped in the same direction every time the conflicting interests have been weighed."[64]

There is another dimension of his concern for consequences, however. As a pragmatist, Stevens tends to shape his holdings to fit the facts of the case at hand. It is inevitable, and from his perspective proper, that his opinions should be written so they might not later be invoked as precedent for cases very different from those at hand. In the franking case, for example, he could predict that no flood of litigation would follow because the decision was limited to the rare circumstance of mass mailings to nonconstituents.[65] In *Nebraska Press Assn. v. Stuart,* in which the Court found unconstitutional a judge's ban on the reporting of information acquired from open court proceedings and public records, among other sources, Stevens wrote a limiting concurrence.

> I agree that the judiciary is capable of protecting the defendant's right to a fair trial without enjoining the press from publishing information in the public domain, and that it may not do so. Whether the same absolute protection would apply no matter how shabby or illegal the means by which the information is obtained, no matter how serious an intrusion on privacy might be involved, no matter how demonstrably false the information might be, no matter how prejudicial it might be to the interests of innocent persons, and no matter how perverse the motivation for publishing it, is a question I would not answer without further argument.[66]

The case should not be understood to establish principles for dissimilar circumstances. He particularizes, in sum, for the sake of both present and future rationality: to make good decisions and to set useful fact-bound precedent. He is critical of unnecessarily broad decisions—freewheeling dictum, for example, and constitutional interpretation where statutory interpretation will do— in part because they extend rulings to situations that have not been adequately considered in court.[67] Good decisions have boundaries.

Pluralism

The force of his concern about rational decision making, with clear rules, ample facts, balancing, and the consideration of likely effects, leads Stevens to pluralism. Sound decisions are not made by appellate judges alone: within their domains, other public and private institutions, from Congress and the lower courts to school and family, have comparable functions, he believes. When they are doing their work well, they deserve the benefit of the doubt, though equally they may expect intervention when their decision making does not adhere to constitutional and statutory standards. The political and social system works better, by and large, when each component is performing the work to which it is best suited.

In an opinion as circuit judge, noted above, in which he defers to a school board's ruling on proper dress and grooming for teachers, Stevens writes:

> It is one thing for us to make judgments upon the ground of rationality in spheres of our own special competence, e.g., whether certain evidence is relevant to a question being litigated, or whether a certain criminal procedure adequately protects the rights of defendants; it is quite another for us to volunteer to assess social problems generally. "There can, of course, be honest differences of opinion as to whether any government, state or federal, should as a matter of public policy regulate the length of haircuts [quoting Justice Black], but it would be difficult to prove by reason, logic, or common sense that the federal judiciary is more competent to deal with hair length than are the local school authorities and state legislatures of all our 50 states."[68]

Some decisions are best made by judges, some by others (particularly if the questions are as trifling as hair length and beards—even if judges were experts on hair length and beards, one more than suspects Stevens would want their time spared for other matters).

In this same case, Stevens quotes Louis Brandeis on a related benefit of pluralism:

> "To stay experimentation in things social and economic is a grave responsibility. Denial of the right to experiment may be fraught with serious consequences to the Nation. It is one of the happy incidents of the federal system that a single courageous State may, if its citizens choose, serve as a laboratory; and try novel social and economic experiments without risk to the rest of the country. This Court has the power to prevent an experiment. We may strike down the statute which embodies it on the ground that, in our opinion, the measure is arbitrary, capricious or unreasonable. . . . But in the exercise of this high power, we must be ever on our guard, lest we erect our prejudices into

legal principles. If we would guide by the light of reason, we must let our minds be bold."[69]

Appellate courts will nurture such pluralism if they generally confine themselves to reviewing authority, competence, and rationality.

Lest it be supposed that his deference to other decision makers is automatic, or nearly so, one may recall the *Groppi* opinion, with which he (and we) began, or any of numerous later cases. A dissent in a deportation proceeding for a former concentration-camp guard is another illustration. Stevens puts down the executive, the court of appeals, and the Supreme Court in one long breath:

> The story of this litigation is depressing. The Government failed to prove its right to relief on any of several theories advanced in the District Court. The Court of Appeals reversed on an untenable ground. Today this Court affirms on a theory that no litigant argued, that the Government expressly disavowed, and that may jeopardize the citizenship of countless survivors of Nazi concentration camps. . . .
>
> . . . I remain firmly convinced that the Court has committed the profoundest sort of error by venturing into the unknown to find a basis for affirming the judgment of the Court of Appeals.[70]

To use the best-known bench mark: Stevens's deference is considerably less predictable than that of Felix Frankfurter, whose words he often cites.

Of the other decision makers, it is to Congress that he is most inclined to defer because of its enormous resources, namely, constitutional authority, information, and political skills. It is far easier to find a federal district judge in error. Not only on questions of congressional authority under Art. I, but even on issues of individual rights that would allow him plausibly to assert the relative expertise of the judiciary, Stevens at times bows to legislative judgment, at least for an initial round of balancing, leaving fine-tuning to the judiciary. For example, in a case in which the Court found constitutional and statutory justification for covert FBI entry of business premises for installation of a legal listening device, Stevens argued in dissent that Congress had not authorized such entries and that the Court should not act in its stead. Congress is better able to weigh facts, evaluate consequences, and decide the complex question whether a new intrusion upon privacy strikes a reasonable balance between individual rights and effective law enforcement. If the rights of the people are to be curbed, Congress should do it, as in the past.[71] In another case he opposed a fixed rule against identifying suspects singly in "show-ups," instead of among others in a traditional lineup. "The rule which is needed is one that can be drafted more effectively by the legislative process than by a somewhat clumsy judicial fiat. . . . The several issues which must be addressed in the formulation of a new rule require more than judicial gloss for adequate resolution," he wrote. "The adoption of a new rule . . . is more appropriately the subject of a legislative decision than of constitutional adjudication."[72]

A more usual form of deference to Congress, for Stevens, is to study the legislative history of a statute in detail in order to adhere faithfully to the lawmakers' will. He does his homework: in a case involving damages against a police officer who gave perjured testimony in a criminal trial, for example, he says:

> This evidence does not . . . tend to show that Congress intended to abrogate witness immunity in civil actions under §1, which applied to wrongs committed "under color of . . . law." The bill's proponents were exclusively concerned with perjury resulting in unjust *acquittals*—perjury likely to be committed by private parties acting in furtherance of a conspiracy—and not with perjury committed "under color of law" that might lead to unjust *convictions*. In hundreds of pages of debate there is no reference to the type of alleged constitutional deprivation at issue in this case: perjury by a *government official* leading to an unjust conviction. Indeed, the legislative history is virtually silent even with regard to perjury by *private* persons leading to convictions of innocent defendants. . . . In several hundred pages of small triple-columned print, only one Senator—not a member of the committee that reported the bill—referred to the possibility that perjury was being used to convict the innocent. His comments were made in connection with a proposal to retain a test-oath for grand and petit jurors.[73]

Most opinions of this kind defy summary or selective quotation, and must be read whole for an understanding of the care Stevens takes to reconstruct the will of Congress from the record.[74]

On the other hand, if a conscientious search turns up little or no coherent legislative purpose, or an absence of serious discussion, deference is unlikely.[75] Dissenting in *Delaware Tribal Business Committee v. Weeks,* he found "manifestly unjust and arbitrary" an act of Congress which, in settling a claim adjudicated by the Indian Claims Commission, provided funds for all but one of the dispersed groups of Delawares covered by the commission's award without rational explanation of the exception. Stevens concluded that the exception was inadvertent: "[T]here is no reason to believe that the discrimination is the product of an actual legislative choice."[76] In dissent in *Fullilove v. Klutznick,* Stevens voted against federal public-works legislation allocating 10 percent of appropriated funds to minority contractors:

> In both its substantive and procedural aspects this Act is markedly different from the normal product of the legislative decisionmaking process. The very fact that Congress for the first time in the Nation's history has created a broad legislative classification for entitlement to benefits based solely on racial characteristics identifies a dramatic difference between this Act and thousands of statutes that precede it. This dramatic point of departure is not even mentioned in the statement of purpose of the Act or in the Reports of either the House or the Senate Committee that processed the legislation, and was not the subject of any testimony or inquiry in any legislative hearing on the bill that was enacted. It is true that there was a brief discussion on the floor of the House as well as in the Senate on two different days, but only a handful of legislators spoke and there was virtually no debate. This kind of perfunctory consideration of an unprecedented policy decision of profound constitutional importance to the Nation is comparable to the accidental malfunction of the legislative process that led to what I regarded as a totally unjustified discrimination in *Delaware Tribal Business Committee v. Weeks.*

> Although it is traditional for judges to accord the same presumption of regularity to the legislative process no mat-

ter how obvious it may be that a busy Congress has acted precipitately, I see no reason why the character of their procedures may not be considered relevant to the decision whether the legislative product has caused a deprivation of liberty or property without due process of law.[77]

His conclusion is that the act is "slapdash" and will not help the disadvantaged. It may assist a favored few within an injured class, but those most in need are the least likely to benefit. The evident purpose, instead, is to give certain congressional constituents "a piece of the action."[78] Normally, however, legislation deserves respect.

Stevens also defers to decision makers in the remainder of the judiciary and in the executive branch, though more cautiously: "Our recognition of Congress' need to vest administrative agencies with ample power to assist in the difficult task of governing a vast and complex industrial Nation carries with it the correlative responsibility of the agency to explain the rationale and factual basis for its decision, even though we show respect for the agency's judgment in both." The asbestos case noted earlier is an example of deference to an administrator—deference, however, only after review of agency procedures and the regulation at issue in the case. Says Stevens, in dissent:

> Because the statute is the Administrator's special province, we should not lightly set aside his judgment. "When faced with a problem of statutory construction, this Court shows great deference to the interpretation given the statute by the officers or agency charged with its administration. 'To sustain the Commission's application of this statutory term, we need not find that its construction is the only reasonable one, or even that it is the result we would have reached had the question arisen in the first instance in judicial proceedings.'"
>
> . . . The wise teaching of Mr. Justice Cardozo . . . is therefore directly pertinent. He observed that an administrative "practice has peculiar weight when it involves a contemporaneous construction of a statute by the men charged with the responsibility of setting its machinery in motion, of making the parts work efficiently and smoothly while they are yet untried and new."[79]

One who is close to the facts, Stevens often argues, is in the best position to know the meaning of the rules. Appellate courts are handicapped by having to deal with incomplete, secondhand facts.

It is a frequent theme in his treatment of the decisions of other courts and a basic reason for his plea, noted in the *Groppi* dissent, that greater confidence be placed in the trial bench, juries, and the bar. For example, he argued that admission to a state bar should be accepted as grounds for admission to practice before the Supreme Court. Unless the Court is willing to provide applicants a fair hearing of its own, it should rely on the considered judgment of the state bar and state courts, who are better able to assess the fitness of their own applicants. Better to rubber-stamp state judgments than to judge from afar in a one-sided proceeding.[80] It is deference no less appropriate to the federal courts of appeals.

> Most certainly, this Court does not sit primarily to correct what we perceive to be mistakes committed by other tribunals. Although our work is often accorded special respect because of its finality, we possess no judicial monopoly on either finality or respect. The quality of the work done by the courts of appeals merits the esteem of the entire Nation, but, unfortunately, is not nearly as well or as widely recognized as it should be. Indeed, I believe that if we accorded those dedicated appellate judges the deference that their work merits, we would be better able to resist the temptation to grant certiorari for no reason other than a tentative prediction that our review of a case may produce an answer different from theirs.[81]

In situations, too, where the soundest decisions are likely to be made by professionals, public and private, or by the family, Stevens's inclination is to defer. Upholding a public hospital's rule against fathers in the delivery room, he says it is doctors, not judges, who can best decide whether a husband's presence is appropriate and safe.[82]

Stevens's thoughts on pluralism and judicial restraint are summarized in a segment of a talk he gave as circuit judge in 1974 at Northwestern University Law School.

> Every decisionmaker, whether he be an umpire at the World Series, a legislator, a corporate manager, a member

of a school board, or a federal judge, is fallible. But if he has earned the right to make decisions through an acceptable selection process, it is safe to predict that most of his decisions will be acceptable. Sometimes he will violate a rule that commands universal obedience, and such error must be corrected. But we should not attach undue importance to the occasional mistake. For the potential error—indeed the inevitable prevalence of a modest amount of error—is an essential attribute of any decisional process administered by human beings.

The prevalence of widespread potential for error among other decisionmakers is one of the factors that repeatedly prompts invitations to federal judges to substitute their views for the erroneous conclusions of others. Sometimes I think federal judges have succeeded in creating an illusion that they are wiser than they really are because their self-imposed limitations on their jurisdiction must have left many losing litigants convinced that if only the federal judge had reached the merits, surely he would have ruled correctly and, of course, the winning litigant knows how wise the judge is. Be that as it may, the temptation to accept an invitation of this kind is always alluring, but whenever the federal judiciary does accept, three things inevitably happen. First, our workload increases and our ability to process it effectively diminishes. . . . Second, the potential for diverse decisions by other decisionmakers is diminished and another step in the direction of nationwide uniformity is taken. . . . And third, we substitute our mistakes for the mistakes theretofore made by others. Sometimes that price is well worth paying; it is, however, a cost of which we should always be conscious.[83]

Synopsis

These, then, are John Paul Stevens's basic principles of judging. From them it is possible to distill several that seem particularly useful to him. (To be sure, no thoughtful judge's procedural preferences can be compressed into a single page, but Stevens's are considerably more straightforward and coherent than most. They lose less in the compression, therefore. Further, the principles are set out at this point with the promise of illustration and elaboration in the substantive chapters that follow.)

1. Judges should keep in mind that they are only one kind of decision maker among many in the social system, each with special responsibilities, skills, and information.
2. Judges are best equipped to apply legal principles to individual disputes, exercising moderate discretion case by case.
3. Appellate judges should make every effort to consider and weigh relevant objective facts.
4. Among such facts are the likely consequences of the judges' decisions, including the benefits and costs of alternative decisions.
5. Both principles and facts are essential: a decision deficient in principle is ad hoc and arbitrary; a decision deficient in fact is unrealistic and mechanical—a "mere formula."
6. In most cases before an appellate court the merits are not all on one side, and judges must balance rather than reach a conclusion by simple deduction.
7. When the balance is close, the court should defer to prior governmental decisions, including judicial precedent, particularly if thoughtfully made.
8. A simple judge-made rule may properly be used to reduce the burden of finding and weighing facts if experience suggests it will directly and substantially serve underlying constitutional and statutory principles.
9. But judge-made rules that oversimplify the points of law and fact relevant to a balanced judgment are to be avoided.
10. Also to be avoided are complex accretions of specific judge-made rules that have proven unfaithful to underlying constitutional and statutory principles or confusing to the public and the legal community, thereby encouraging unprincipled, ad hoc decision making.

Origins

Most members of the modern Court, when it comes to choosing, favor ideology over strongly pragmatic, pluralistic rules of deci-

sion such as these. Even so, the pragmatic moderates are an unusually able group, have swing votes to cast in close cases, which
are many, and are therefore influential beyond their numbers.
Among them none has practiced the pragmatist's trade more dil-
igently and lucidly than Stevens. He shares much with his fellow
moderates, but he has also defined a role of his own on the Court.

It is interesting that the pragmatism which sets Stevens apart
from his brethren on the Supreme Court, in varying degrees,
places him in the mainstream of American jurisprudence. In
wider context it is the committed liberals and conservatives on
the Court who are out of step. The reasons are familiar. First,
presidents regard the Supreme Court as a policymaker on a par
with the executive and legislative branches and tend to name
justices for their liberalism or conservatism; by contrast, in appointments to circuit and district courts, which are usually governed by senatorial courtesy, considerations of ideology and policy
often give way to local forces of patronage. (The Reagan administration, which has made an effort to impose ideological screen-
ing at all levels, is the exception.) Second, intermediate and lower
federal courts have less freedom to act ideologically than the Supreme Court, which can claim the last word in constitutional litigation and dampen the other courts' enthusiasm for ideological
excursions.

Below the level of the Supreme Court, judges are more likely to
build upon the legal wisdom of the past—the Constitution, acts
of Congress, and judicial precedent—than to engage in forward-
looking liberal or conservative social engineering (in which liberals envision a society with less repression, poverty, ignorance,
pollution, and the like; conservatives less antisocial behavior,
welfare dependency in the broadest sense, and regulation of business; and both sides apply judicial activism or restraint tactically
to these ends). The role of the district and circuit courts is mainly
to decide cases with reference to existing policy; the Supreme
Court is more overtly devoted to making and remaking constitutional policy.

John Paul Stevens is a Supreme Court justice whose way of
thinking about cases is essentially the same as it was on the court
of appeals.[84] He remains a jurist without a social agenda; he is
not a partisan or an ideologue. He has seen himself, as judge and
justice alike, as a problem solver, a member of one component of
a decision-making system in which no one has, or should have,

the last word. Significantly, Stevens has been known from the start as a "legal craftsman" and "judge's judge," terms of honor within the legal community suggesting a good mind, mastery of the law, and a sense of place. In these respects he has most resembled an Eisenhower appointee, Potter Stewart.

President Eisenhower, distressed at the wayward liberalism of his first Supreme Court appointee, Earl Warren, governor of California and presidential hopeful, decided to name people with experience on federal courts or state supreme courts thereafter.[85] A judge's record, he thought, correctly, was likely to offer a good basis for predicting his behavior on the Supreme Court. Whittaker, who soon left the Court, Harlan, and Stewart decided cases according to expectation; Brennan, a highly regarded liberal Democratic state judge, named by Eisenhower with the 1956 election in mind, was a second disappointment, but in his case there was fair warning in the record. On the whole, the requirement of judicial experience worked as Eisenhower intended. Eight of Franklin Roosevelt's nine appointees, by contrast, were without significant judicial experience and proved to be as unpredictable a lot, at least on questions of individual rights, as any in the Court's history.

Thus, if a president wants a moderate pragmatist, he can choose from a large pool on the federal or state bench, though to find one of the caliber of Stewart or Stevens is a challenge. And if he wants a fairly predictable liberal or conservative with judicial experience, he can find one of them, too, though the pool is smaller. Thurgood Marshall and Sandra Day O'Connor are examples (both with service on an appellate court, both strongly ideological, and of course both chosen in part as symbolic "firsts" on the Court—the first black and the first woman). Even Justice Blackmun stayed on the intended conservative track for a number of years after his promotion to the high court before beginning his migration leftward.

Those who have known Stevens well and followed his career have predicted his approach to judging with great accuracy. It is a career that goes in a straight line from college to the Supreme Court, each effort bringing success and recognition, encouraging him on to the next: at the University of Chicago he was an outstanding student, joined a fraternity, edited the school paper, won the university's highest honors for scholarship and campus activities, and graduated Phi Beta Kappa in 1941.[86] One of the very few signed pieces he wrote for the paper, the *Daily Maroon,* aside from fraternity news, an April 1940 column entitled "Peace Strikes Are Silly," contains strong intimations of his style on the bench decades later. It is a moderate's appeal for fact-finding, debate among contending factions, the importance of means as well as ends, and particularistic decision making based on principle *in context* (text reprinted in endnote).[87] Under his direction the paper ran long essays by senior members of the faculty on various sides of the public issues of the day. It was an unusually sophisticated policy dialogue for a college paper, even for the *Daily Maroon* at the University of Chicago in the days of the Great Books. It, too, presages his later insistence upon openness and rationality.

He was decorated for service in the navy during the war that ensued; and at Northwestern University Law School he became editor-in-chief of the law review, graduating first in his class. He served as clerk to Supreme Court justice Wiley Rutledge, 1947–48; was in private practice in Chicago, 1948–52; and served as associate counsel of a Senate subcommittee studying monopoly power, 1951; as a partner in a Chicago law firm, 1952–70; as a member of the Attorney General's committee to study antitrust laws, 1953–55; as a lecturer at Northwestern University Law School, 1953, and the University of Chicago Law School, 1954–55; as a general counsel to an Illinois commission investigating the conduct of state supreme court justices, 1969; as a judge of the United States Court of Appeals, 1970–75; and as a Supreme Court justice from 1975 on.[88]

What Stevens did in college and thereafter worked. He had no reason to develop alternative ways of thinking about the world or shift course toward other lawyerly pursuits. He continued to rely on his scholarly powers of analysis and written expression, which had served him well in his formative years. He wrote articles, a chapter in a University of Chicago volume on justices of the Supreme Court, lectured, and took stints of government service calling for legal analysis. His later reputation as a legal craftsman thus was long in the making.

Something else one notes in his chronology is the relative absence of partisanship and political causes. Even when party affiliation was a factor in his appointment to a study commission and later to the federal bench, it was not in reward for political activity or in expectation of partisan service. (In contrast, most federal circuit court appointees have been quite prominently active in partisan politics.)[89] Indeed, his appointment as general counsel to a commission investigating judicial impropriety bespeaks a reputation for neutrality and objectivity.

All in all, for those who knew his work, there can have been no surprise that Stevens was both skilful and objective on the bench, emphasizing rationality over substantive goals. It was the kind of record that allowed old, admiring friends to recommend him with confidence for the court of appeals and, five years later, the Supreme Court. Charles Percy, onetime classmate at the University of Chicago, having become a moderate Republican member of the United States Senate, proposed him for the federal circuit court of appeals in 1970. Early in his first term, Senator Percy, intent upon improving the quality of federal judicial appointments from Illinois, emphasizing merit over politics, had arranged for competition among the bar associations in the area to suggest the names of outstanding candidates as vacancies occurred. Writes Percy:

> Out of that process came John Paul Stevens. At the time of his nomination, the process brought forward—out of scores of candidates—the names of three potential nominees for my personal review and interview. One of them was listed as "J. P. Stevens". I had not seen John in years and when I interviewed him as a potential nominee for the vacancy that had occurred in the Circuit Court of Appeals, he urged that I hold off at least five years in submitting his name or even putting the question to him because he had children to educate and also had not achieved the goals that he had established for himself or his law firm.
>
> I said to him, as I recall, "John, in five years I don't know whether we'll still have a Republican president to whom I can submit names, and besides, by then you should be thinking in terms of moving on to the Supreme Court" (at which point I crossed my fingers behind my back). Whichever argument was more convincing I am not sure, but my arguments had their effect. He gave me his approval to submit his name.[90]

In 1975 Senator Percy was joined by Attorney General Edward Levi, formerly of the University of Chicago, a friend of the Ste-

vens family, in recommending Stevens's elevation to the Supreme
Court. He was a lawyer's lawyer when nominated to the court of
appeals, said Percy, and now a judge's judge.[91]

In that year the *Chicago Tribune* could describe Stevens as "a
steady judge and a good one," not once reversed by the Supreme
Court in five years on the appeals court. It said:

> For too long the Supreme Court has been divided between
> relatively inflexible blocs—the liberal activists on the one
> side and the conservatives on the other. As the usual
> "swing" members, Justices Stewart and White have had
> more influence than any two men should. If Judge Stevens'
> nomination is confirmed, he will become a third member
> of this influential group and will thereby strengthen the
> court.[92]

Then, as always, those who knew his record had been able to fore-
cast Stevens's role as a judge. Senator Percy reflects:

> John Paul Stevens always was a master of any subject
> that he tackled. He had what they call a "judicial temper-
> ament" even as a college student. He had a brilliant, curi-
> ous mind, constantly probing and digging for the truth,
> whatever the issue. He worked hard but was never a
> "grind". He had deep feelings about searching for facts,
> studying the philosophers of old as well as the thoughts
> and lives of the founders of our constitutional form of gov-
> ernment. He had an interest in politics but never, to my
> knowledge, with the intention of becoming a politician. He
> had a deep desire to seek the truth; he was willing to listen
> to every point of view, then seemed to be able to make a
> decision as to which point of view he felt correct without
> internal struggle. He lived in a neighborhood struggling to
> provide equal rights for all men and women regardless of
> color, and there is a consistency to his views, written as
> well as orally expressed, through the years. Of the scores
> of nominations that I have made of federal judges through
> my 18 years in the Senate, he is certainly the one who
> meant the most personally to me and in whom I have had
> the greatest pride.[93]

All of the direct and indirect observations, in different eras, seem to match.

That along with his scholarly habits and political moderation Stevens should have acquired a pragmatic concern for facts and consequences is no surprise. In the years of his young adulthood, pragmatism was in the air—over the country, the universities, and particularly the law schools. Anyone who studied law in the 1940s, certainly in one of the better schools, was heavily exposed to pragmatism and to criticism of traditional jurisprudence, as unintentionally caricatured by Justice Roberts in 1936:

> When an act of Congress is appropriately challenged in the courts as not conforming to the constitutional mandate, the judicial branch of the Government has only one duty,—to lay the article of the Constitution which is invoked beside the statute which is challenged and to decide whether the latter squares with the former.[94]

The moderate pragmatism of working attorneys and judges, exemplified by Louis Brandeis, was a staple for all law students. One of Stevens's teachers at Northwestern, Nathaniel Nathanson, had clerked for Brandeis, who pioneered the use of factual appellate briefs in support of the constitutionality of state welfare legislation. As a judge, Brandeis was also known as a legal technician of the first order, concerned about procedures and the bounds of judicial activity, as in his concurrence in *Ashwander v. TVA*.[95]

Stevens was also directly affected by legal realism, a pragmatic reform movement of the 1920s and 1930s which culminated in the radical rule-skepticism of Jerome Frank, echoing Oliver Wendell Holmes, Jr.'s assertion that "general propositions do not decide concrete cases." One of Stevens's professors, Leon Green, a leading realist, whom Stevens describes as having had a special influence on his understanding of the law,[96] considered legal rules greatly overrated. Rules, particularly simple formulas, he said, are likely to strangle rather than guide the thought of judges and to confuse juries—though he conceded there might be some reason to allow jurors to be fooled into thinking they worked. Green believed that a judge is on his own, by and large, deciding cases according to good policy as he conceives it, assembling precedent as needed to justify his decisions. His opinions are unlikely to show how decisions are actually made, Green said. Judges judge, inevitably, but they write opinions that give an impression of passivity and deference to rules and precedent.[97]

To make the best of their discretion, Green suggested that judges use wisdom—a philosophy of law based on "life at large," reflecting the "experience of the ages," an eclectic formulation like Cardozo's. Green, along with a number of legal realists, also had some faith in the application of science to problems of law, perhaps the least enduring of the realists' beliefs. Further, Green stressed fact. "A principle must rest upon the facts from which it was deduced." Legal principles by themselves, without facts, are dicta. The doctrine of *stare decisis* must be constrained by distinguishing fact situations and avoiding the application of precedent to dissimilar circumstances.[98]

Green was critical of the pre-1937 Court and strongly endorsed Franklin Roosevelt's court-packing plan, not by the traditional logic of consistency with the language or original intent of the Constitution, to be sure, a phantom issue to thoroughgoing legal realists, but on the theory that judges should keep the Constitution in tune with the development of the nation. The Court is and should be a political branch of government, whose members interpret the Constitution in the light of the desires and interests of the people. He regarded the gradual growth of the Constitution via interpretation as both logically and practically superior to formal amendment, which is difficult, slow, and results in a "highly crystallized formula" that itself requires interpretation in individual cases before it can be understood.[99]

Nathaniel Nathanson was Stevens's first constitutional-law professor. He, too, was skeptical of abstractions and supportive of court packing; he favored broad interpretation of the commerce power of the national government and of individual rights.[100]

For both Green and Nathanson the work of the Court was not so much to send legal signals outward to society from the Constitution and the bench as to accept legislative and adjudicative facts from the outside in order to keep the Constitution in gear with the social and economic order.

There is some similarity between Stevens's rules of decision and the views of Green and Nathanson: rules are never so clear as to absolve judges from exercising judgment; at their worst, rules impede rational judgment; one must emphasize facts and experience; one must be aware of the interests at stake in litigation. But Stevens did not fully accept legal realism: he is not nearly as skeptical of rules; he does not regard law as even potentially scientific; and though he is conscious of the judiciary as no more than an element in a larger political and social system, he stresses the special competence of courts to interpret and apply law (and of the political branches to reflect the will of the people) rather than seeing all three branches as similarly political.

Stevens learned the lessons of radical realism, and in the end settled for half a loaf: some new ideas, some old; some modern skepticism and distaste for formalism, tempered by an old-fashioned faith in principles; some wish to keep up with the times, but a solid respect, too, for the tried and true. Many others have accepted this compromise, in effect giving up naive faith in certainty in the law without renouncing law itself, recognizing that judges necessarily have great discretionary authority and the challenge to use it wisely.[101] It is Cardozo, Frank, Brandeis, and others together. Even though it is not the view of most members of the Supreme Court, it is the modern consensus in American law.

Stevens went from law school and Dean Green to the Supreme Court to clerk for a former dean, Wiley Rutledge, who among other things sharpened his concern for the rights of individuals. Stevens's open, pragmatic, and eclectic view of the law was well formed when he left for his clerkship. It was a view that emphasized the need to consider the interests affected by decisions. What Rutledge did was reinforce his pragmatic tendencies and increase his sensitivity to liberal values. Stevens remained a process-minded moderate, but his vision of the interests at stake was widened.

The best evidence that Stevens's moderation and pragmatism, which characterize his circuit court and Supreme Court opinions, were formed much earlier in life is a chapter, quoted above, that he wrote on Wiley Rutledge in 1956, in his mid-thirties. It is a sensitive analysis of the work of Justice Rutledge, but on balance a better guide to the thinking, years later, of Judge and Justice Stevens. In his hands, Rutledge becomes first and foremost an apostle of moderation and judicial restraint, a champion of individual rights secondarily. Stevens notes that, "appropriately," Rutledge's first and last opinions as Supreme Court justice *rejected* claims of individual rights, which might lead one to regard Rutledge as a good deal less than the complete liberal the voting statistics show him to have been on individual rights, second only among his contemporaries to Frank Murphy and well ahead of William Douglas. Stevens emphasizes Rutledge's

—skepticism about the mechanical application of general rules, particularly simple formulas, a skepticism moderated by a profound faith in the rule of law;[102]
—belief that judges inevitably judge, and judge best when they apply the distilled wisdom of institutional and personal experience;[103]
—appetite for facts;[104]
—practicality;[105]
—awareness of the good and bad effects of judicial decisions, including undue burdens on the courts themselves;[106]
—tendency to review every aspect of a case, painstakingly, "to see the merit in both sides of a controversy," and to discuss his findings and conclusions in separate opinions;[107]
—deference to other decision makers: to other judges in the litigation at hand, to other courts and Congress by scholarly exploration of precedent and legislative history, and to administrative agencies, but in every instance with a watchful eye for abuses.[108]

The list contains every item in Stevens's own rules of decision, above, more or less explicitly, with one exception: Stevens's aversion to complex, unhelpful accretions of judge-made rules. But the worst instances of undue complexity, in Stevens's view, came well after the writing of the chapter on Rutledge, in rulings on obscenity, the establishment of religion, and the equal protection of the laws.

Thus Stevens's approach to judging was firmly in mind before he took the bench and has stuck. This is not to say that his thinking is rigid. What *is* rigid is his practice, in every case, of examining consequences with care and striving for clarity, objectivity, and balance. Substantively, he is demonstrably *less* rigid than most justices. We shall examine his approach in the contexts of the First Amendment, due process of law, and equal protection in Chapters 2, 3, and 4, and in Chapter 5 draw comparisons with other members of the Court.

2

The First Amendment

Above all, First Amendment cases display Justice Stevens's preference for balancing, in contrast with the majority's reliance on less flexible forms of decision. In every application of the amendment, except to religious establishment questions, he assesses countervailing interests and assigns weights according to circumstance. Thus even in decisions on the First Amendment, where absolutistic answers have generally been more common than in other areas of the Constitution, he balances.

Options

There are different ways of balancing, however, not equally acceptable to Stevens. It is useful, therefore, to begin with a definition of major alternatives as he sees them, including nonbalancing approaches. (Since there is not much agreement in his opinions or in the general literature on labels for these approaches, I have supplied a working set—part his, part mine, part others'—to make distinctions between Stevens's approach and those of other members of the Court, past and present. The labels refer to ranges along a continuum, not to discrete forms of decision.) Briefly:

(Generalizing)   Absolutism
                        Simple Balancing
        ↑   Compound Balancing
        ↓   Case-By-Case Balancing
(Particularizing)   Ad Hoc Decision

Of these, simple and compound balancing are most often used by the modern Court.

Stevens rejects the extremes of unprincipled ad hoc decision making and absolutism alike, although he approaches the latter on questions of establishment of religion.[1] He believes neither that the Court should decide cases concerning expression and religion without reliance on the principles of the Constitution nor that the words "Congress shall make no law" require the Court to prohibit all constraints upon freedom of expression and religion. Most appellate judges would concur; they are balancers, too.

But while pure absolutism is not favored by American judges, something rather like it is: simple or definitional balancing, which results in the application of constitutional principles to some subjects and not to others and allows judges mechanically to uphold some kinds of claims and reject others, may equally be viewed as a form of absolutism. Judges who decide that an expression is obscene and therefore without constitutional protection may be reasoning absolutistically (the First Amendment protects all speech whatsoever, but obscenity is not speech) or balancing categorically (obscenity is speech of so little value that societal interest in its regulation may be assumed to outweigh the individual's interest in free expression).[2] If there is balancing in such cases, it is a priori. The merits are all or nearly all on one side. Once the questioned law or practice has been categorized, the outcome is certain; the judges need not concern themselves with contextual detail.

Compound balancing, less perfunctory, follows from the view that a given case involves more than one constitutional interest, or more than one dimension of a single interest, no one of which may be assumed in advance to outweigh the other or others combined. An approximate value on the order of high, medium, or low is assigned to political debate, let us say, or to commercial advertising, imparting some degree of ease or difficulty to the task of proving the governmental restriction in question unconstitutional. The value assigned is neither so high nor so low, however, as to determine the outcome as in simple balancing. The value of political expression is high, for example, but it may be outweighed by national security interests in some instances, though perhaps not by a community's desire for peace and quiet in its public park on a Sunday afternoon.

Case-by-case balancing, in the sense of the direct application of a broad-gauge constitutional principle to the full facts of a case, often without mediating subprinciples, is exemplified by the question whether due process has been accorded in a state trial. It is an approach for which one remembers Felix Frankfurter, who disliked categories; it is now less often observed in appellate courts than in trial courts. In a sense, case-by-case balancing is the limiting instance of compound balancing, in which two or more variables are balanced, though in case-by-case balancing the categories are at most implicit, unlimited in number, and assessed more by impression than by weighing. Since case-by-case balancing is more characteristic of due process than First Amendment litigation, however, it too may be put to one side without impairing our analysis of Justice Stevens and the Court on the freedom of religion and expression. The live options, again, are simple and compound balancing; the others are exceptional.

In First Amendment cases, the Court engages in both kinds of balancing. On establishment of religion and free speech and press questions, the majority of the members tend to rely on simple balancing; in free exercise of religion cases, by contrast, the Court is more inclined to particularize with compound balancing. Stevens tends to use the latter in all kinds of First Amendment litigation, though less so in establishment cases. His is a more consistent preference for fact-gathering and individualizing, though not to the point of doing without explicit judge-made categories.

There are two kinds of First Amendment issues on which Stevens may appear absolutistic: government aid to religious schools and the prosecution of obscenity. In fact, his reasoning is more complex in both; there is indeed an element of absolutism in the former, however, though not in the latter. Exploring these exceptions, real and apparent, helps put his general tendency toward particularization and balancing in perspective.

Establishment of Religion

The Court's simple balancing in cases of government aid affecting church schools and on other establishment questions is in the form of a three-part test: "[A] legislative enactment does not contravene the Establishment Clause if it has a secular legislative purpose, if its principal or primary effect neither advances nor inhibits religion, and if it does not foster an excessive government entanglement with religion."[3] A law that crosses any one of these lines is unconstitutional. But as long as the three-part test is satisfied, some linkage of church and state is allowed. (Were the three factors weighed against one another, the test would be an instance of compound balancing. But there is no internal weighing; the balancing is of establishment, so defined, against the benefit of government assistance, and the latter always loses once an establishment is discovered.)

Earlier, the Supreme Court employed a much less complex test of religious establishment. When the words "Congress shall make no law respecting an establishment of religion" were considered by the Court for the first time, in 1947, in *Everson v. Board of Education,* they were given an interpretation derived from the views of Thomas Jefferson and James Madison. In an opinion by Hugo Black, the Court said, "In the words of Jefferson, the clause . . . was intended to erect 'a wall of separation between church and State.'" With respect to financial support the Court said, "No tax in any amount, large or small, can be levied to support any religious activities or institutions, whatever they may be called, or whatever form they may adopt to teach or practice religion." The dissenting opinion of Wiley Rutledge is similar (agreeing with the Court's statement of constitutional principle but disagreeing on whether the principle should apply to government reimbursement of bus fares for children attending parochial schools): "The prohibition broadly forbids state support, financial or other, of religion in any guise, form or degree. It outlaws all use of public funds for religious purposes."[4]

It was a position enjoying the support of early dictum if not of authoritative precedent. In 1878, in *Reynolds v. United States,* a polygamy case, the Court had quoted Jefferson:

"Believing with you that religion is a matter which lies solely between man and his God; that he owes account to none other for his faith or his worship; that the legislative powers of the government reach actions only, and not opinions,—I contemplate with sovereign reverence that act of the whole American people which declared that their legislature should 'make no law respecting an establishment of religion or prohibiting the free exercise thereof,' thus building a wall of separation between church and State."[5]

The thread was broken in the second half of this century, however, with the adoption of the purpose-effect-entanglement test. To Stevens, the abandonment of the Jeffersonian view in cases involving government aid to religious education was a misfortune. "This Court's efforts to improve upon the *Everson* test have not proved successful," he has written. "'Corrosive precedents' have left us without firm principles on which to decide these cases." The Court has instead resorted to ad hoc decisions, "groping for a rationale," and the states have been given an incentive to invent new ways of circumventing the law.[6] His exasperation is evident:

> [T]he entire enterprise of trying to justify various types of subsidies to nonpublic schools should be abandoned. Rather than continuing with the sisyphean task of trying to patch together the "blurred, indistinct, and variable barrier" described in *Lemon v. Kurtzman,* I would resurrect the "high and impregnable" wall between church and state constructed by the Framers of the First Amendment.[7]

Both the Court and Stevens are fairly rigid about establishment of religion, then, though their definitions of establishment differ: Stevens's is broader and simpler. Clearly, however, he does not believe that legislation is foreclosed simply by the statement of the First Amendment that Congress shall make "no law" on the subject, because as we shall see he willingly accepts varying degrees of regulation of all the other subjects included in the amendment, governed by the same two words. His view is the view of the framers of the amendment, as he understands it, supported by *Reynolds* and *Everson*, including the separate opinion of Wiley Rutledge, rather than a literal interpretation as such.

Beyond the lessons of legal history, however, there are pragmatic considerations of importance to Stevens. In one case, it is true, he declined to argue relative merit with those who stressed the benefits of government aid. "Though such subsidies might represent expedient fiscal policy," he said, "I firmly believe they would violate the Establishment Clause. . . ." In another, however, he assesses the adverse effects of state aid on sectarian colleges, notably, "the pernicious tendency of a state subsidy to tempt religious schools to compromise their religious mission" by secularizing parts of their curricula in order to qualify for subsidy. "The disease of entanglement may infect a law discouraging wholesome religious activity as well as a law encouraging the propagation of a given faith." State aid may work against religion and, to put it in broader context, against cultural pluralism.[8]

Other evidence of pragmatic concerns on the establishment question may be seen in his opinion for the court of appeals in 1973 in a case involving the consolidation of public-school districts into a larger district to be served by a former Catholic school, not the government-aid issue in the cases above. Stevens found that on balance the school, leased from the diocese by the public-school system and renamed, was operating in accord with the First Amendment. There were no more religious services and classes or religious artifacts, fewer nuns in the classroom, and fewer Catholic books and magazines in the school library. But the plaintiffs contended that the school had a religious presence still. Their evidence was that all members of the school board were Catholic, the school was located by a Catholic convent, most of the teachers were Catholic and a number of them nuns, some paintings depicting religious themes were still hung in the school, and some members of the faculty exhibited a "Catholic attitude." On the other hand there was evidence that the students had succeeded in minimizing conflict, that by court order the nuns were to cease wearing their habits in class, and that balance was being brought to the library and the display of art.

> The evidence abundantly establishes the reasonableness of the decision to close the old facility at Birdseye; the consolidation was certainly within the Board's power. We accept the sincerity of plaintiffs' concern about the assimilation of their children into a group of students predominantly of a different faith and recognize that subtle influences may be impermissible even though difficult to prove by objective evidence. Nevertheless, we are persuaded that

the appropriate remedy in this case lies not in the direction of a return to the outdated facility at Birdseye, but rather in the direction of unambiguous and vigilant enforcement of the commands of the First Amendment at the modern, integrated school in Ferdinand. Indeed, if the manner in which the Ferdinand school is operated violates the Establishment Clause, the reopening of Birdseye would, instead of terminating the violation, probably perpetuate it.

The end of separation of church and state is resolutely affirmed in this opinion, but the reasoning with regard to implementation is a model of factual inquiry, compound balancing, and concern for consequences.[9]

The theme that Stevens most emphasizes in establishment cases, however, is that the Court's own formula is hopelessly complex and muddled. Rather than making the meaning of the clause clearer and more easily enforceable than it would be by itself, the Court's accretion of imprecise tests has made it difficult for legislators and judges to know what is lawful and what is not. It has drawn them from principled discretion, for want of clear rules of law, into ad hoc decision making. Stevens's views of religious establishment reflect his concern that judge-made rules be practicable as well as historically accurate. He values logic and clarity for their own sake, and his own opinions are tight and lucid. But it is more than logic: as a pragmatist, he wants judges' decisions to work, and for that their written opinions must be understandable. Other things being equal, the simpler rule is the more workable. It may be a broad constitutional provision ("no person shall . . . be deprived of life, liberty, or property without due process of law," for example) or a specific rule designed to limit judicial or police discretion, such as the guarantee of free counsel for indigent defendants. The Court's test of establishment of religion, however, is neither simple nor workable: it has the look of clarity; in practice it is a puzzle.

Obscenity

In the same spirit, Stevens rejects the Court's increasingly complex reasoning in obscenity prosecutions. The constitutional question was first squarely posed the Court in 1957 in *Roth v. United States* and *Alberts v. California* as "whether obscenity is utterance within the area of protected speech and press."[10] The Court decided it was not, citing dictum in the seminal "fighting words" case, *Chaplinsky v. New Hampshire:* "There are certain well-defined and narrowly limited classes of speech, the prevention and punishment of which have never been thought to raise any Constitutional problem. These include the lewd and obscene. . . ."[11] Obscenity, said the Court, is "utterly without redeeming social importance." The old English test, the effect of isolated passages upon the most susceptible persons, was abandoned in favor of a new one: "whether to the average person, applying contemporary community standards, the dominant theme of the material taken as a whole appeals to prurient interest."[12] It is a complex definition, but like the three-part test of religious establishment an example of "simple" balancing: anything that fits its terms is unconstitutional; other variables are irrelevant. The balancing is a priori. *Roth-Alberts* proved to be a test more easily stated than applied, however. Thurman Arnold, arguing for a magazine distributor in a Vermont court, said it best: "The spectacle of a judge poring over the picture of some nude, trying to ascertain the extent to which she arouses prurient interest, and then attempting to write an opinion which explains the difference between that nude and some other nude has elements of low comedy." The case law was of little help, said Arnold—he knew of no more unedifying writing in American law. Rather than try to divine the meaning of "obscenity" and justify their conclusions in writing, he mused, courts might better simply find publications and other expressions obscene or not without explanation.[13] Justice Stewart adopted this approach, which is "unprincipled" in this chapter's neutral sense, in his well-known concurrence in 1964:

> It is possible to read the Court's opinion in *Roth v. United States* and *Alberts v. California* in a variety of ways. In saying this, I imply no criticism of the Court, which in those cases was faced with the task of trying to define what may be indefinable. I have reached the conclusion, which I think is confirmed at least by negative implication in the Court's decisions since *Roth* and *Alberts,* that under the First and Fourteenth Amendments criminal laws in this

area are constitutionally limited to hard-core pornography.
I shall not today attempt further to define the kinds of material I understand to be embraced within that shorthand
description; and perhaps I could never succeed in intelligi-
bly doing so. But I know it when I see it. . . .[14]

The majority, however, though at times deciding obscenity
cases without opinion in this period, typically struggled to clarify
its position by refining and re-refining the *Roth-Alberts* test. In
Memoirs v. Massachusetts in 1966, for example, the Court said
that "three elements must coalesce: it must be established that
(a) the dominant theme of the material taken as a whole appeals
to a prurient interest in sex; (b) the material is patently offensive
because it affronts contemporary community standards relating
to the description or representation of sexual matters; and (c) the
material is utterly without redeeming social value."[15]

In 1973, in *Miller v. California,* the Court adopted still another
version, less friendly to First Amendment claims:

The basic guidelines for the trier of fact must be: (a)
whether "the average person, applying contemporary community standards" would find that the work, taken as a
whole, appeals to the prurient interest; (b) whether the
work depicts or describes, in a patently offensive way, sexual conduct specifically defined by the applicable state law;
and (c) whether the work, taken as a whole, lacks serious
literary, artistic, political, or scientific value.

The Court also said in this case that the "community" mentioned
in the test need not be the nation. Some variation in the meaning
of obscenity would be permitted from place to place.[16]

Such was the law when Stevens joined the Court. It was not
long before he found an opportunity to criticize the *Miller* test. In
Liles v. Oregon, he concurred with the majority in denying certiorari, but only, he explained, for want of enough votes to both
take the case and proceed to remove the judiciary from the business of punishing obscene expression. The *Liles* case involved
prosecution for the sale of motion picture films under a criminal
statute written to conform to the language of the *Miller* opinion.
As long as the Court favored retention of *Miller,* said Stevens,
there was no point in endlessly rearguing and reaffirming.[17]

His criticism of the majority view was that it failed to give lower federal and state courts the standards they needed to decide cases with any consistency and any degree of predictability.[18] He cited the dissenting opinion of William Brennan, joined by Potter Stewart and Thurgood Marshall (a total of four votes, including his own—one short of the five required to overturn *Miller*), containing statements by the trial judge displaying the capriciousness that results from inadequate guidance by the Supreme Court:

> Well, what is patently offensive?
> And, frankly, I had to kind of apply my own standard, which, I believe, corresponds with the standards of the community. And the standard probably, simply stated and boiled down, is the same one that was taught to me by my mother from the day I was a small child. If there was something of which I would not want her to know, then don't do it. Pretty simple.
> Applying that standard I would think that I wouldn't get any quarrel out of anyone in this room, that they wouldn't want their mothers sitting next to them while they looked at either one of these movies.

But Stevens would vote to deny certiorari in such cases for the time being, "in the interest of conserving scarce law library space. . . ."[19]

The following year, in a case accepted for full argument, he explained his discontent with criminal obscenity prosecutions at greater length.

> There are three reasons which, in combination, persuade me that this criminal prosecution is constitutionally impermissible. First, as the Court's opinion recognizes, this "statute regulates expression and implicates First Amendment values." However distasteful these materials are to some of us, they are nevertheless a form of communication and entertainment acceptable to a substantial segment of society; otherwise, they would have no value in the marketplace. Second, the statute is predicated on the somewhat illogical premise that a person may be prosecuted criminally for providing another with material he has a

constitutional right to possess. Third, the present constitutional standards, both substantive and procedural, which apply to these prosecutions are so intolerably vague that evenhanded enforcement of the law is a virtual impossibility. Indeed, my brief experience on the Court has persuaded me that grossly disparate treatment of similar offenders is a characteristic of the criminal enforcement of obscenity law.

How, he asked in a footnote, can a reviewing court tell whether a jury knows what the standards of the community are? [20]

Dissenting shortly thereafter in *Smith v. United States,* a case in which the Court upheld a conviction for the mailing of obscene material under the Comstock Act of 1873, Stevens was still more explicit, calling for a principled reexamination of the premises of recent cases, particularly the "community standards" and "patently offensive" elements of *Miller v. California.* His position, to begin with, is that federal law forbidding obscenity in the mails should be administered uniformly throughout the land: neither a federal criminal statute nor, certainly, the First Amendment should have different meanings in different parts of the country. He regards it as a point that went without saying until the Court's acceptance of the community-standards test in the *Roth-Alberts* case. [21]

Furthermore, what is "obscene" or "offensive" is hard to define even within a single community, even in the unlikely event of agreement on the boundaries of the community to be considered. In the confusion, jurors and judges tend to lapse into subjectivity. [22] Stevens concludes that the line between offensive and inoffensive expression is too blurred for identification of criminal conduct, to say nothing of the limits of First Amendment protection. [23]

(Not long after, in *Ward v. Illinois,* Stevens considered another requirement of *Miller v. California,* that the law as written or construed specifically define the offensive conduct in question. In his view, the requirement of specificity was a reasonable element in an otherwise unfortunate line of thought; he deplored the fact that the majority no longer took it seriously.) [24]

The Court's position on obscenity prosecutions, then, like its rulings on government aid to church schools, excites Stevens's

aversion to murky judge-made formulas. But in obscenity cases
such as *Smith v. United States* there is an element not present in
establishment cases, namely, criminal prosecution: "Petitioner
has been sentenced to prison . . . ," he begins his dissent in that
case.[25] The confused state of the law of criminal obscenity creates
a risk of severe punishment for actions that are not clearly unlawful. Stevens concludes that criminal prosecution is inappropriate
for regulating the sale of erotic material.[26] If the regulation is
civil, however, the constitutional objection is less substantial. No
individual interest approaching the importance of not being sent
to jail for an ill-defined crime is at stake in a question, let us say,
of whether an adult movie theater may be barred from a residential area. A flexible standard may even have positive value in
civil law: "Although the variable nature of a standard dependent
on local community attitudes is critically defective when used to
define a federal crime, that very flexibility is a desirable feature
of a civil rule designed to protect the individual's right to select
the kind of environment in which he wants to live."[27] In the context of obscenity cases generally, Stevens's approach to criminal
obscenity is seen, then, as an instance of compound balancing:
obscenity has degrees of offensiveness (thus society's variable interest in its suppression), and sanctions vary from civil penalties
to imprisonment (thus the individual's variable interest in well-
defined rules).

Balancing of this kind is evident also in *New York v. Ferber,* a
rare obscenity case in which Stevens argues support of criminal
prosecution—of a pornographer who used children as the subjects
of lewd movies. The weight of the state's interest in preventing
the sexual abuse of children is so great that criminal sanctions
may properly be imposed on those who profit from such films, he
wrote, taking care to distinguish this kind of case from the general run of obscenity prosecutions.[28] In his concurrence, however,
he objects to a blanket rule even with respect to child pornography:

> Assume that the operator of a New York motion picture
> theater specializing in the exhibition of foreign feature
> films is offered a full-length movie containing one scene
> that is plainly lewd if viewed in isolation but that never-
> theless is part of a serious work of art. If the child actor
> resided abroad, New York's interest in protecting its young

from sexual exploitation would be far less compelling than in the case before us. The federal interest in free expression would, however, be just as strong as if an adult actor had been used.[29]

To summarize: a common element in Stevens's opinions on establishment of religion and obscenity prosecution is an objection to complex, unworkable judge-made law. A secondary concern is pluralism. His response in each case is a clear prohibition—of establishment and of the criminal prosecution of obscenity, narrow exceptions aside. But the reasons are different. With respect to establishment of religion, pragmatic considerations merely reinforce a legal-historical conclusion that the framers meant this clause of the First Amendment, perhaps this clause alone, to be taken absolutely or nearly so. In the case of criminal obscenity, despite a conclusion that initially seems equally broad—an end to prosecution—the underlying logic is different: there is no absolutistic historical interpretation, but instead a genuine compound balancing of First Amendment and, in effect, due process concerns. Stevens is uncompromising only on certain establishment questions.

On other First Amendment issues, his balancing is evident throughout. It is compound balancing, assigning different weights not only to the government interest in regulation from case to case, but to different kinds of expression as well. He is not the first to advocate variable First Amendment values, but he does so with rare consistency.

We shall first examine expression of relatively low value.

Compound Balancing I

In his confirmation hearing Stevens was asked just how the Court goes about deciding First Amendment cases today. Does it balance? Should it balance? He replied,

I think even in the First Amendment area, there is some balancing that must be done because cases . . . do not arise in neat pigeonholes. There is a question as to whether what is regulated is merely the time and place of speaking as opposed to the content of speaking. And there is quite a different approach depending upon what kind of issue is raised.

You have to look both at the interest of the speaker and the public interest in having the communication become a part of the public domain. There are various factors and I think you will find in my opinions some recognition of both sides of the public interest in communication.[30]

Earlier in the hearing he had said that he placed a very high value on the amendment, as have many members of the Court in recent decades, of course, none more deliberately than Wiley Rutledge. Nevertheless, Stevens always recognizes contrary concerns. To a question about the collision of First Amendment and other interests, he responded that even this basic right would yield to the needs of national security on occasion. He added, ". . . I would think . . . perhaps when a particular case comes up I might find I have spoken somewhat loosely, without sufficient reflection, but my general reaction would be that A, [the government] bears a heavy burden, and B it bears some burden of factual presentation to enable a factfinder to know that this is not merely a formula of words that is being used to justify something other than a real national security interest."[31]

Stevens's penchant for balancing, as distinguished from more rigid approaches to decision, can be seen clearly in civil obscenity cases. Here as in First Amendment cases generally he employs a sliding scale of values for various kinds of speech, the merits to be determined in good part by the facts of the case at hand. Erotic expression, like commercial speech, as we shall see, is at the lower reaches of his scale.[32] It is valued less than political debate, let us say; how much less cannot be said in terms both universal and precise. Stevens rejects the Court's all-or-nothing test: obscenity is not entirely unprotected by the Constitution, in his view, since it should not ordinarily be criminally punishable, nor is nonobscene erotic material wholly protected.

In *Young v. American Mini Theatres,* in the portion of his opinion supported by a majority of the members, Stevens says that "there is surely a less vital interest in the uninhibited exhibition of material that is on the borderline between pornography and artistic expression than in the free dissemination of ideas of social and political significance. . . ."[33] In Part III, with the vote of a plurality only, Justice Powell having taken exception, Stevens elaborates his argument that nonobscene erotic expression has some, but not much, constitutional value.

> [E]ven though we recognize that the First Amendment will not tolerate the total suppression of erotic materials that have some arguably artistic value, it is manifest that society's interest in protecting this type of expression is of a wholly different, and lesser, magnitude than the interest in untrammeled political debate that inspired Voltaire's immortal comment. Whether political oratory or philosophical discussion moves us to applaud or to despise what is said, every schoolchild can understand why our duty to defend the right to speak remains the same. But few of us would march our sons and daughters off to war to preserve the citizen's right to see "Specified Sexual Activities" exhibited in the theaters of our choice. Even though the First Amendment protects communication in this area from total suppression, we hold that the State may legitimately use the content of these materials as the basis for placing them in a different classification from other motion pictures.[34]

That being so, an ordinance restricting the location of adult movie theaters in order to preserve neighborhoods may well be unobjectionable. In this case an interest in protecting the quality of city life deserves high respect.[35] With low value on one side of the balance and a weighty public interest on the other, the conclusion perforce is that the regulation is constitutional. He reasons similarly in cases involving nude dancing.[36]

In *FCC v. Pacifica Foundation,* the Court faced the question whether the federal government has the power to regulate broadcasting that is indecent but not obscene, in this instance a recording by George Carlin entitled "Filthy Words," featuring seven common words referring to "excretory or sexual activities or organs," as the Court put it, in a twelve-minute monologue broadcast over the radio. The program was inadvertently tuned in by a man driving in his car with his young son. The father complained to the Federal Communications Commission, which ordered that the complaint be placed in the file where it might be used against the station at license renewal time.

Stevens's opinion, in part for the Court and in part for himself, the Chief Justice, and William Rehnquist, justified government regulation with compound balancing. In the majority portion, he notes it is not a criminal case; if it were, as we have seen, he would almost surely vote against the government. In the plurality portion, he assigns the language of the monologue low constitutional value, as in his plurality opinion in *Young v. American Mini Theatres.*

> If there were any reason to believe that the Commission's characterization of the Carlin monologue as offensive could be traced to its political content—or even to the fact that it satirized contemporary attitudes about four-letter words— First Amendment protection might be required. But that is simply not the case. These words offend for the same reasons that obscenity offends. Their place in the hierarchy of First Amendment values was aptly sketched by Mr. Justice Murphy when he said: "[S]uch utterances are no essential part of any exposition of ideas, and are of such slight social value as a step to truth that any benefit that may be derived from them is clearly outweighed by the social interest in order and morality."[37]

But there are countervailing considerations:

> Although these words ordinarily lack literary, political, or scientific value, they are not entirely outside the protection of the First Amendment. Some uses of even the most offensive words are unquestionably protected. Indeed we may assume, *arguendo,* that this monologue would be protected in other contexts. Nonetheless, the constitutional protection accorded to a communication containing such patently offensive sexual and excretory language need not be the same in every context. It is a characteristic of speech such as this that both its capacity to offend and its "social value," to use Mr. Justice Murphy's term, vary with the circumstances. Words that are commonplace in one setting are shocking in another.[38]

He continues, once again for a majority of the Court:

> This case does not involve a two-way radio conversation between a cab driver and a dispatcher, or a telecast of an Elizabethan comedy. We have not decided that an occasional expletive in either setting would justify any sanction or, indeed, that this broadcast would justify a criminal prosecution. The Commission's decision rested entirely on a nuisance rationale under which context is all-important. . . . As Mr. Justice Sutherland wrote, a "nuisance may be merely a right thing in the wrong place,— like a pig in the parlor instead of the barnyard." We simply hold that when the commission finds that a pig has entered the parlor, the exercise of its regulatory power does not depend on proof that the pig is obscene.[39]

He is concerned about "context," and that means the medium and its implications.

Compound balancing with expression of little weight on one side of the balance may also be seen in Stevens's treatment of commercial speech. Until 1975 the Court accorded commercial speech no First Amendment protection. Then in *Virginia State Board of Pharmacy v. Virginia Citizens Consumer Council* it was given some, but not the degree enjoyed by most other speech.[40] In other words, the Court abandoned simple protected/not-protected balancing and adopted a compound-balancing approach. (With respect to obscenity, however, the majority has held more or less to the view that obscenity is unprotected by the Constitution and nonobscene sexual expression is protected—held to it except in joining the brief discussion in Stevens's opinion in *Young,* quoted above, but not in the more explicit passage that follows. Stevens's position is more consistent: he rejects simple balancing with respect to obscenity and commercial speech both.)

In cases involving commercial speech, Stevens's compound balancing assigns the expression low weight in general and different levels of protection in different contexts. Graffiti and ear-splitting sounds in advertising are examples of commercial expression a community might quite lawfully not only regulate but ban if it asserted a contrary interest.

His differences with the Court are only a matter of degree in this area: the Court is flexible about commercial speech; Stevens is more so. The flexibility may be noted in the definition of commercial speech itself. Of the opinion of the Court in *Central Hudson Gas & Electric v. Public Service Commission,* he writes:

> Because "commercial speech" is afforded less constitutional protection than other forms of speech, it is important that the commercial speech concept not be defined too broadly lest speech deserving of greater constitutional protection be inadvertently suppressed. . . .
>
> In my judgment one of the two definitions the Court uses in addressing that issue is too broad and the other may be somewhat too narrow. The Court first describes commercial speech as "expression related solely to the economic interests of the speaker and its audience." Although it is not entirely clear whether this definition uses the subject matter of the speech or the motivation of the speaker as the limiting factor, it seems clear to me that it encompasses speech that is entitled to the maximum protection afforded by the First Amendment. Neither a labor leader's exhortation to strike, nor an economist's dissertation on the money supply, should receive any lesser protection because the subject matter concerns only the economic interests of the audience. Nor should the economic motivation of a speaker qualify his constitutional protection; even Shakespeare may have been motivated by the prospect of pecuniary reward. Thus, the Court's first definition of commercial speech is unquestionably too broad.[41]

He continues, with more examples to give meaning to general terms:

> The Court's second definition refers to "'speech proposing a commercial transaction.'" A salesman's solicitation, a broker's offer, and a manufacturer's publication of a price list or the terms of his standard warranty would unquestionably fit within this concept. Presumably, the definition is intended to encompass advertising that advises possible buyers of the availability of specific products at specific prices and describes the advantages of purchasing such items. Perhaps it also extends to other communications that do little more than make the name of a product or a

service more familiar to the general public. Whatever the precise contours of the concept, and perhaps it is too early to enunciate an exact formulation, I am persuaded that it should not include the entire range of communication that is embraced within the term "promotional advertising."

(Fellow moderate Harry Blackmun also concurs in the judgment. He, however, pursues clarity by traditional logical analysis of precedent rather than the more pragmatic definition-by-enumeration.)[42]

In *Bolger v. Youngs Drug Products Corp.*, he is equally concerned that the Court not classify as commercial any speech deserving greater constitutional protection. In this case, a condom manufacturer had sent advertisements unsolicited through the mail, with literature detailing the symptoms and effects of venereal disease as well as a discussion of family planning. The statute invoked by the Postal Service prohibits the mailing of "[a]ny unsolicited advertisement of matter which is designed, adapted, or intended for preventing conception." Stevens concludes that the mailings have a significant noncommercial component and must be accorded the protection they would have if they were wholly noncommercial.[43]

Stevens's separate opinions in *Carey v. Population Services International* and *Metromedia, Inc. v. San Diego* deal directly with the relative value of commercial speech.[44] In *Carey*, which among other things tested a state law banning advertisements of contraceptives, he drew directly on his balancing of interests in obscenity litigation.

The fact that a type of communication is entitled to some constitutional protection does not require the conclusion that it is totally immune from regulation. Cf. *Young v. American Mini Theatres, Inc.* (opinion of Stevens, J.). An editorial and an advertisement in the same newspaper may contain misleading matter in equal measure. Although each is a form of protected expression, one may be censored while the other may not.

In the area of commercial speech—as in the business of exhibiting motion pictures for profit—the offensive character of the communication is a factor which may affect the time, place, or manner in which it may be expressed. Cf.

> *Young.* The fact that the advertising of a particular subject
> matter is *sometimes* offensive does not deprive all such ad-
> vertising of First Amendment protection; but it is equally
> clear to me that the existence of such protection does not
> deprive the State of all power to regulate such advertising
> in order to minimize its offensiveness. A picture which may
> appropriately be included in an instruction book may be
> excluded from a billboard.[45]

The elements of compound balancing are there: speech of varying
importance and of varying degrees of offensiveness, from which
derive degrees of legitimate public interest in regulation.

Justice Stevens, dissenting in part, enlarged upon his view of
commercial speech in *Metromedia,* in which the court struck
down an ordinance prohibiting certain kinds of outdoor advertising. He joined a section of the plurality opinion asserting that in
various applications the values of the First Amendment must
give way to other interests, but supplied his own illustrations,
which included the wish of the community not to suffer graffiti or
loud and raucous noises.

> It seems to be accepted by all that a zoning regulation ex-
> cluding billboards from residential neighborhoods is justi-
> fied by the interest in maintaining pleasant surroundings
> and enhancing property values. The same interests are at
> work in commercial and industrial zones. Reasonable men
> may assign different weights to the conflicting interests,
> but in constitutional terms I believe the essential inquiry
> is the same throughout the city. For whether the ban is
> limited to residential areas, to the entire city except its
> most unsightly sections, or is citywide, it unquestionably
> will limit the quantity of communication. Moreover, the
> interests served by the ban are equally legitimate and sub-
> stantial in all parts of the city. Those interests are both
> psychological and economic. The character of the environ-
> ment affects property values and the quality of life not only
> for the suburban resident but equally so for the individual
> who toils in factory or invests his capital in industrial prop-
> erties.[46]

(He finds no fault with an exemption for political campaign signs
in the San Diego ordinance: ". . . I must assume that these signs

may be just as unsightly and hazardous as other offsite billboards. Nevertheless, the fact that the community places a special value on allowing additional communication to occur during political campaigns is surely consistent with the interests the First Amendment was designed to protect.")[47]

Compound Balancing II

If he assigns advertisements and sexual expression limited weight in the balance, there are other communications, involving political or public issues, that Stevens values considerably more, as his remark about political billboards suggests. Their protection by the First Amendment helps make democracy work.[48] Stevens dissented from a decision of the Court in 1980, for example, which allowed the removal of an Air Force Reserve officer from active duty for circulating a petition on a military base without permission of the base commander. The majority found the Air Force requirement that permission be sought consistent with both the First Amendment and a federal statute proscribing unwarranted restrictions on the communication of service personnel with members of Congress. Stevens saw no need to resort to the Constitution to decide the issue: the evident purpose of the statute "to remove impediments to the flow of information to Congress" in the spirit of the First Amendment was enough to resolve any specific doubt whether Congress intended to protect the circulation of petitions.[49]

His approach to cases involving the right of prisoners to communicate with people outside the prison walls is similar, even though the relation of prisoners' mail to the democratic process is less direct than the circulation of petitions aimed at legislators:

> Whether we view the issue from the standpoint of the prisoner's right to communicate with others, or from the standpoint of society's right to know what is happening within a penal institution, it is perfectly clear that traditional First Amendment interests are at stake. . . .
>
> Before a democratic society can effectuate drastic institutional changes, the community at large must be in-

formed about the need for change. That there is inadequate public awareness of the nature of our penal system, and that the system as a whole needs to be changed dramatically, are propositions which correctional officials are not likely to challenge. . . . If the reasons for our faith in the principles embodied in the First Amendment are valid, it is not unreasonable to infer that there is a causal connection between those two propositions.[50]

In another but rather different prison case, involving access of the press, Stevens, again dissenting, reaffirms the value of expression in the service of democracy. In *Houchins v. KQED, Inc.,* a broadcasting station sought access to a county jail where an inmate's suicide had drawn attention to substandard conditions. According to the majority of the Court, the First Amendment does not guarantee a right of access to sources of information within government control. Stevens counters, "The preservation of a full and free flow of information to the general public has long been recognized as a core objective of the First Amendment to the Constitution. It is for this reason that the First Amendment protects not only the dissemination but also the receipt of information and ideas."[51] He cites Alexander Meiklejohn:

"Just so far as . . . the citizens who are to decide an issue are denied acquaintance with information or opinion or doubt or disbelief or criticism which is relevant to that issue, just so far the result must be ill-considered, ill-balanced planning, for the general good. *It is that mutilation of the thinking process of the community against which the First Amendment to the Constitution is directed."*[52]

And James Madison:

"A popular Government, without popular information, or the means of acquiring it, is but a Prologue to a Farce or a Tragedy; or, perhaps both. Knowledge will forever govern ignorance: And a people who mean to be their own Governors, must arm themselves with the power which knowledge gives."[53]

And adds:

> It is not sufficient, therefore, that the channels of commu-
> nication be free of governmental restraints. Without some
> protection for the acquisition of information about the op-
> eration of public institutions such as prisons by the public
> at large, the process of self-governance contemplated by
> the Framers would be stripped of its substance.
>
>   For that reason information gathering is entitled to
> some measure of constitutional protection. As this Court's
> decisions clearly indicate, however, this protection is not
> for the private benefit of those who might qualify as repre-
> sentatives of the "press" but to insure that the citizens are
> fully informed regarding matters of public interest and im-
> portance.[54]

The constitutional basis of these assertions? He concedes there is
no right to receive or acquire information in the words of the Constitution, but the specific guarantees of the Bill of Rights have no
force if the necessary means of implementation are not guaran-
teed as well—if they are not considered fundamental themselves.
The marketplace of ideas is a barren place if there are willing
participants but no information to buy or sell.[55]

It is a short step to the right of the public and the press to attend
criminal trials. Stevens's position has been that the Sixth Amendment guarantee of a public trial is a right enjoyed by the accused
rather than the public—a right that the accused may waive,
therefore—but that the public and press have a right to access
under the First Amendment, a position he forthrightly describes
as a new rule of law. In 1980 he voted with the majority to reverse
a murder conviction in a trial from which the public and press
had been excluded. Concurring, he wrote, "This is a watershed
case. Until today the Court has accorded virtually absolute protection to the dissemination of information or ideas, but never
before has it squarely held that the acquisition of newsworthy
matter is entitled to any constitutional protection whatsoever."[56]
As a pragmatist, in short, he has championed the extension of the
First Amendment to the gathering as well as the dissemination
of information on questions of public concern. (Moderates Stewart
and Blackmun, each concurring in the judgment, arrive at the

same conclusion in opinions leaning more toward precedent and legal history.)[57]

Yet as a pragmatist Stevens particularizes and balances. He rejects the argument that news gathering has an absolute priority, in every case, over the defendant's right to a fair trial. Concurring in the judgment in *Nebraska Press Assn. v. Stuart,* which overturned a judicial order restraining the publication of accounts of confessions or facts "strongly implicative" of the accused in a sensational mass murder case, Stevens held to the same position: firm affirmation of First Amendment rights coupled with a refusal to concede that in another time and place those rights might not give way to even weightier contrary interests.[58] He would not join Brennan's absolutistic concurrence, therefore, though he agreed with much of it.

Of all the controversies involving public issues or political expression, none has found Stevens weighting the First Amendment more heavily than those in which he has attacked political patronage. In 1972 he led the Court of Appeals for the Seventh Circuit, and in 1980 the Supreme Court, to the view that requiring a person to be a member of a given party to obtain or keep a non-policy-making appointive government position is violation of the guarantees of the First Amendment.[59]

It is possible to see his position in these cases as a logical extension of precedent in closely related areas. It is equally possible to view it as judicial policy-making in the raw. (Lewis Powell, dissenting in *Elrod v. Burns,* for example, objects that "[t]he Court holds unconstitutional a practice as old as the Republic, a practice which has contributed significantly to the democratization of American politics. This decision is urged on us in the name of First Amendment rights, but in my view the judgment neither is constitutionally required nor serves the interest of a representative democracy. It also may well disserve—rather than promote—core values of the First Amendment.")[60]

What Stevens has argued, first as circuit judge, is that firing a lower-level government employee for membership in a party out of power is as much a violation of the First Amendment as not renewing the contract of a teacher in a municipal junior college because of his criticism of the college administration or requiring government employees to profess their loyalty by denying past association with Communists, both of which have been condemned by the Supreme Court. "We think it unlikely that the

Supreme Court would consider these plaintiffs' interest in freely associating with members of the Democratic party less worthy of protection than the Oklahoma employees' interest in associating with Communists or former Communists."[61] As a member of the Supreme Court he did not participate in *Elrod v. Burns,* but in 1980 he wrote the opinion of the Court in *Branti v. Finkel,* a similar case, and reaffirmed his early view of patronage. That patronage dismissals may be temporary, since one's party is likely to make a comeback sooner or later, that the promise of appointment is a source of party strength and therefore, arguably, an ingredient of democracy, and that in any event it is an old tradition, are considerations insufficient to overcome the damage to First Amendment rights. "While the patronage system is defended in the name of democratic tradition, its paternalistic impact on the political process is actually at war with the deeper traditions of democracy embodied in the First Amendment." In this as in other cases of speech and association in the realm of politics, the rights of the person usually outweigh the demands of the government, in Stevens's view. Some loss of government efficiency, in not hiring as freely as a private employer, is a small price to pay for liberty.[62]

Conclusion

Stevens's approach to freedom of speech questions is to distinguish communications of greater and lesser value and to weigh each against the public interest in constraint, which varies according to context, as in his pig-in-the-parlor opinion in *FCC v. Pacifica Foundation.* Because it is commonplace in Stevens's opinions, the compound balancing of pigs and parlors is a good summary point. It also offers an opportunity to consider his provocative assertion that the government may regulate speech according to its content (i.e., pigs *versus* people).

In the face of forceful contrary views, Stevens insists that content is a normal and proper consideration in framing constraints upon speech. In 1980, in *Consolidated Edison Co. v. Public Service Commission,* the Court overturned a state regulation banning utility bill inserts that discussed controversial issues, in this instance nuclear power and national energy independence. Said the Court, "A restriction that regulates only the time, place, or manner of speech may be imposed so long as it is reasonable. But when regulation is based on the content of speech, governmental action must be scrutinized more carefully to ensure that communication has not been prohibited 'merely because public officials disapprove the speaker's views.' As a consequence, we have emphasized that time, place, and manner regulations must be 'applicable to all speech irrespective of content.'"[63]

Stevens, concurring in the judgment, would allow the inserts, but for different reasons. He begins with an academic analogy: "Any student of history who has been reprimanded for talking about the World Series during a class discussion of the First Amendment knows that it is incorrect to state that a 'time, place, or manner restriction may not be based upon either the content or the subject matter of speech.'"[64]

"There are, in fact," he continues, "many situations in which the subject matter, or, indeed, even the point of view of the speaker, may provide a justification for a time, place, and manner regulation. Perhaps the most obvious example is the regulation of oral argument in this Court; the appellant's lawyer precedes his adversary solely because he seeks reversal of a judgment. As is true of many other aspects of liberty, some forms of orderly regulation actually promote freedom more than would a state of total anarchy." Shortly he makes it clear, however, that not all regulation of content is unobjectionable: "A regulation of speech that is motivated by nothing more than a desire to curtail expression of a particular point of view on controversial issues of general interest is the present example of a 'law . . . abridging the freedom of speech, or of the press.' A regulation that denies one group of persons the right to address a selected audience on 'controversial issues of public policy' is plainly such a regulation."[65] In the case at hand, the state thought customers might find the message offensive, an impermissible ground. Had the offensiveness been in the "form" of the communication, as he puts it—via loudspeaker, for example, or excessively ugly in a given setting, as were the seven dirty words on daytime radio—the regulation might have been sustained. But here it was the thought itself the state found offensive, and the regulation thus violated the First Amendment.

Despite this confrontation, which entails some overstatement on both sides, Stevens and the Court are in basic agreement. Both would allow reasonable regulation of the time, place, and manner of expression. The regulation is not reasonable in the eyes of the Court if it is based on content; in Stevens's view, on the contrary, content may be a proper basis of regulation—even content, he says, in the sense of point of view. Yet in his example of oral argument before the court, he describes mere "rules of the road"— time, place, and manner regulations based not on favoritism for one point of view at all but on assuring each side its time in court on an equal footing. It is not what is usually regarded as regulation according to point of view. In short, in describing regulation that does and does not involve approval or disapproval as based on "content," Stevens only muddies the waters and makes himself appear less friendly toward the First Amendment than he really is. (It might be less misleading to avoid the highly ambiguous term "content" altogether, to use "point of view" for situations in which approval or disapproval is implied, and to save "subject matter" for the rest, with at least a modest presumption that restrictions based on point of view are unconstitutional and on subject matter, not. Some lawful time, place, and manner regulations will be based on "subject matter," as in the scheduling of oral arguments in court; and some will not, as in the case of the raucous loudspeaker cited by Stevens or, better, of such a loudspeaker in a residential neighborhood at three in the morning, which presumably would be adjudged identically whether the noise consisted of a reasoned political address or popular music.)[66]

Examples from academia present some complications, however. The World Series *versus* the First Amendment, in *Consolidated Edison,* may be seen as a straightforward time, place, and manner question: if it is the time and place for discussion of the First Amendment, baseball is an inappropriate topic, as the First Amendment would likely be in a seminar on the theory of baseball in the gymnasium. But there may also be some implication that the First Amendment is a worthier subject of university study than baseball, and thus some approval or disapproval. The point is clearer in *Widmar v. Vincent,* in which Stevens concurred in the judgment as in *Consolidated Edison.* "In performing their learning and teaching missions, the managers of a university routinely make countless decisions based on the content of communicative materials. They select books for inclusion in the library, they hire professors on the basis of their academic philosophies, they select courses for inclusion in the curriculum, and they reward scholars for what they have written. In addition, in encouraging students to participate in extracurricular activities, they necessarily make decisions concerning the content of those activities."[67]

The question in *Widmar* was whether a state university might deny campus facilities used by student organizations generally to a registered religious group on the ground that the campus may not be used for religious worship or religious teaching. In making a decision to create an open, public forum for student groups, said the Court, the university incurred an obligation to be even-handed, not to discriminate unconstitutionally against any one group. A forum need not be created, but once it is, the Constitution takes over. The exclusion in this case was found to violate the First Amendment guarantees of free speech and free exercise of religion, specifically "the fundamental principle that a state regulation of speech should be content-neutral. . . ."[68]

In his separate opinion, Stevens expressed concern that characterizing a state university's student activities program as a public forum and putting a heavy burden on the state to justify any content-based regulation of speech in that forum might unduly constrain the judging of content that is a constant obligation of a university.

> Because every university's resources are limited, an educational institution must routinely make decisions concerning the use of the time and space that is available for extracurricular activities. In my judgment, it is both necessary and appropriate for those decisions to evaluate the content of a proposed student activity. I should think it obvious, for example, that if two groups of 25 students requested the use of a room at a particular time—one to view Mickey Mouse cartoons and the other to rehearse an amateur performance of Hamlet—the First Amendment would not require that the room be reserved for the group that submitted its application first. . . . In my opinion, a university should be allowed to decide . . . whether a program that illuminates the genius of Walt Disney should be given precedence over one that may duplicate material adequately covered in the classroom.[69]

Public universities *are* different from other governmental institutions; they *do* judge quality at every step. Professors are expected to discriminate against weak arguments in a way no chief of police may discriminate, under the First Amendment, in dispensing parade permits. In *Widmar* and in the opening hypothetical analogy in *Consolidated Edison,* Stevens offers unrepresentative cases, therefore, of little use in judging more ordinary regulations impinging on speech. Though he says that a university "may not allow its agreement with the viewpoint of a particular speaker to determine whether access to a forum will be granted," he also does not regard most university gatherings as part of the public forum, subject to the rules of strict neutrality.[70] (Surely a university should be open-minded about divergent points of view in all of its forums, public or not, but Stevens does not make that argument.)

The academic setting apart, then, the differences between Stevens and the Court on the regulation of speech according to "content" are not as great as they appear in *Consolidated Edison* and *Widmar.* The differences, as the cases illustrate, are of degree. Stevens prefers compound to simple balancing and thus does more weighing. In *Consolidated Edison* the communication is a highly valued "expression of a particular point of view on controversial issues of general interest" in an inoffensive setting; in *Widmar* the communication is valued as a contribution to "the intellectual life of a university" in a favorable setting.[71] By contrast, the expression in *Pacifica* is of considerably less value and unusually offensive in a context in which it is imposed unannounced on an unwilling, impressionable audience.

For Stevens, most First Amendment cases follow the rule that good judicial decisions are balanced decisions.

3

Due Process of Law

The main ingredients of Justice Stevens's due process opinions are three: respect for the principle, a sense of its costs as well as its benefits, and deference to lower courts and other primary decision makers. Like freedom of expression, due process is a guarantee not to be applied abstractly but with an eye to facts and context: All things considered, was the decision fair? What is the cost of overturning an otherwise unobjectionable decision because of procedural irregularity? What is to be gained by due process in this case? Is the claim raised in defense of a substantial interest? Has the appellate court time to consider such cases? Are the factual questions ones it can handle as capable as a trial court or an administrator? Concerns such as these underlie Stevens's reluctance to extend formal due process requirements to minor administrative decisions and his view that due process is better achieved by trial courts than by appellate courts, which should intervene sparingly. Even so—to put this in perspective—his voting record is more liberal than the average of all other members of the Court on civil and criminal due process questions together, as we shall see in Chapter 5, and among the moderates on the Court he is clearly the most supportive of the procedural rights of criminal defendants.

Deference to Trial Courts

Since those with the best information make the best decisions, in Stevens's view, primary decision makers deserve the benefit of the doubt on review. If they are administrators, or even legislators, as in *Groppi v. Leslie,*[1] the usual due process questions are whether they should themselves provide some of the forms of due process, typically notice and a hearing before a neutral party, and whether their decisions should be reviewed by the courts to see if existing due process requirements have been followed. In criminal and civil disputes originating in trial courts, closeness to the facts combines with neutrality and procedural sophistication to create a high likelihood of fair treatment, according to Stevens. The questions courts ask of administrative decision making, concerning internal remedies and the appropriateness of review, need not often be asked of courts: the main question is how much deference appellate courts should accord trial courts. For Stevens, the answer is a great deal.

The elements of deference set out in Stevens's opinions are not novel; they are commonplaces of American jurisprudence. But he is unusually faithful to them, often in dissent against an appellate-court majority for whom judicial restraint in this context is a less constant principle. If his conditions for deference are met, he defers willingly.

In *United States v. Smith,* in an early dissent noted in Chapter 1, Stevens criticized fellow circuit judges for imposing an unduly confining rule on trial judges, who in his opinion have the ability to exercise fair and informed discretion. ("Fundamental fairness may require discussion of certain important consequences in specific cases, but a rigid rule that makes a guilty plea vulnerable whenever a trial judge fails to supplement counsel's advice with an enumeration of all significant consequences of the plea is neither necessary to the maintenance of civilized standards of procedure nor desirable.")[2] His dissent not long after in *United States v. Thomas* again illustrates his faith in the trial judge. Thomas, a lawyer, was convicted of sending insurance companies false claims through the mails, accompanied by doctors' and hospital bills for clients who were either uninjured or less seriously injured than Thomas claimed. After the verdict, a juror complained of a newspaper report of the matter that had been seen and dis-

cussed by jurors as they approached a decision against the defendant. It said, "Dr. Pope [who had pleaded guilty and was a witness
for the prosecution in Thomas's trial] was indicted with Thomas
and five other attorneys in the alleged insurance padding which
caused three million dollars in losses to several insurance companies." The other jurors signed a statement supporting the complaint. To the circuit court the article seemed to suggest that the
defendant was part of a larger conspiracy, involving more people
and far more money than alleged in the trial. The court thought
the judge should have queried the jurors about the effect of the
report on their decision.[3]

Stevens disagreed. Since the jury had already rendered its verdict when its exposure to the article was brought to the judge's
attention, the damage could not be undone. It is true, the judge
might have conducted a limited investigation of the truth of the
jurors' statement, had that seemed necessary; otherwise it remained only to decide whether he had abused his discretion in
deciding that the article was insufficiently prejudicial to require
a new trial. Precedent, said Stevens, allows a trial judge a large
discretion on questions of prejudice in cases of this sort. "Generalizations beyond that statement are not profitable, because each
case must turn on its special facts."[4] Even in the cold case record
one finds substantial support for the judge's decision, based on his
observation of the demeanor and testimony of witnesses, not to
hold a new trial.[5] The opinion illustrates a number of Stevens's
themes from Chapter 1, notably, full facts, particularization, and
deference (after satisfying himself that the judge's decision was
well made).

Still looking over the judge's shoulder to be reasonably certain
that deference is appropriate *in this case,* Stevens concludes that
the trial judge is in a better position than the appellate judge to
assess the facts developed at trial.

> Defendant's guilt is starkly apparent. Moreover, the sub-
> stance of the news story was brought to the jury's attention
> by defense counsel. On cross-examination Dr. Pope ac-
> knowledged that similar referrals from other personal in-
> jury lawyers provided him with his major source of income
> and that he saw between 30 and 40 patients per day. He
> evaded defense counsel's question about "a number of other
> indictments." The record developed by defendant thus in-

dicated, if it did not explicitly describe, the existence of wide-spread insurance padding by Dr. Pope and lawyers other than defendant which had resulted in the return of several indictments.

The theory of the defense was that defendant was not a participant in the scheme, or, more narrowly, that the specific charges against him had not been proved beyond a reasonable doubt. This defense, though not contradicted by the news story, may well have been prejudiced by the estimate that insurance padding amounted to $3,000,000. I find it difficult to assess the extent of the prejudice; I am persuaded, however, that the probability of significant prejudice is not plain enough to warrant disagreement with the contemporaneous evaluation made by an experienced trial judge. Indeed, even disagreement with a discretionary ruling would not establish error.

Almost every jury trial requires some compromise with standards of absolute perfection; such deviations must be tolerated if the jury system is to function effectively. In my opinion the trial judge did not abuse his discretion in concluding that the deviation reflected by this record was within permissible limits.[6]

To Stevens these are practical realities, not theory. Concurring in the judgment in *United States v. Hasting,* he depicts the frustration of trying, and failing, in the time available, to re-create the human reality of a trial from a transcript:

I have spent several hours reviewing the one copy of the trial transcript that has been filed with the Court. But I have not read all of its 1,013 pages, and I have read only a few of the 450 pages of the transcript of the suppression hearing. The task of organizing and digesting the testimony is a formidable one. The victims' testimony refers to the perpetrators by various descriptions—"the one with the goatee," "the tall one," "the skinnier one," "the heavier set one," "the bigger one," "a stocky, heavy set guy," "the fat one," "the short, thinner one," "the one in the big hat," "the guy with the hair out," "the guy with the fro," the "shorter one with short hair," the "skinnier one with the shorter hair," "a younger guy," "the guy with the smudged up nose," "the smashed nose," "the ones that was in the back"—rather than by name. As a practical matter, it is impossible for any Member of this Court to make the kind of conscientious and detailed examination of the record that should precede a determination that there can be no reasonable doubt that the jury's deliberations were not affected by the alleged error.[7]

(He then argues for a decision on other grounds.) Deference is especially appropriate in close cases. In a civil rights suit he writes, "We shall not describe the evidence of discrimination except to note that it was marginal; whichever way the trial judge had ruled, his determination of that issue would not have been clearly erroneous."[8]

Stevens is most critical of appellate courts that, not content simply to check the quality of lower-court decisions, try to redo the decisions themselves. For example, in *United States v. Lovasco,* in which the majority of the Supreme Court rejected constitutional objections to a delay in an indictment, Stevens in dissent stressed that the purported reason for delay—to take time for an investigation—was based on unsworn argument at the appellate level rather than the record below. There was no evidence in the transcript of the reasons for the delay. Appellate courts, he said, have no business making decisions on the basis of unsworn matter outside the formal record. In this case the majority of the members of the Supreme Court, the court of appeals, and the district court were on one side, Stevens on the other; but he considered the decision making below sufficiently flawed to merit a dissent.[9]

Fact-finding in a trial court often involves an assessment of the credibility of witnesses, something an appellate court is hard-pressed to do from a cold record. In the Federal Rules of Civil Procedure, the Supreme Court admonishes, "Findings of fact shall not be set aside unless clearly erroneous, and due regard shall be given to the opportunity of the trial court to judge the credibility of the witnesses." Stevens willingly complies. "We are not inclined to make a fresh appraisal of the credibility of witnesses whom the trial judge saw and heard."[10]

In other cases, the issue is whether to interfere with procedural judgments. For instance, with respect to a district judge's decision to use grand jury transcripts from one case in another, Stevens was troubled by the Court's inflated view of the appellate function. "Whatever its validity, the decision of the District Judge as affirmed by the Court of Appeals was surely not very wide of the mark. Accordingly, for the Court to overturn that decision is to move decisively in the direction of equating an 'abuse of discretion' with an exercise of discretion with which it disagrees. I cannot join in this rearrangement of the respective roles of trial and appellate courts."[11]

A recurrent line of reasoning by Stevens in criminal and civil cases alike is that fairness is a quality of the trial as a whole, not of its parts. Thus in *Bachner v. United States,* which raised a question of the validity of a plea of guilty by one not told of a mandatory parole term to follow release from prison, Stevens commented, in concurrence, that the majority's holding that the record disclosed no "fundamental defect which inherently results in a complete miscarriage of justice" was in effect a statement that the proceedings, in this instance on arraignment, viewed as a whole, were not fundamentally unfair. Minor errors in the judge's advice to the defendant do not render a judge's acceptance of a guilty plea unconstitutional, particularly if the defendant has been represented by competent counsel. (The other side of that sentiment appears in a later case: "Some constitutional rights . . . are so basic to a fair trial that their infraction can never be treated as harmless error. In my opinion the right to the effective assistance of counsel at trial is such a right.")[12]

In *United States v. Trutenko,* like *United States v. Thomas* a circuit court case concerning use of the mails for insurance fraud, Stevens, in an opinion of the court this time rather than in dissent, again voted to affirm a conviction despite a large flaw in the proceedings. The prosecutor undoubtedly had erred with an appeal to the pecuniary interest of the jurors as premium payers. "Whenever an error like this occurs, a strong argument for reversal can be made. Reversal would have the salutary effect of deterring similar prosecutorial misconduct in the future. In each case, however, we must evaluate the importance of error in the context of the entire trial before deciding to reverse."[13] Stevens explains why reversal is unwarranted in this case: sufficient evidence of guilt; the improper remark aside, a dispassionate and well-reasoned argument by the prosecutor; a possibility that the comment actually helped as well as hurt the defendant by impugning the character of government witnesses; little likelihood that an isolated remark about relatively little money would prejudice jurors; the absence of objection by counsel; and fair instructions to the jury by the trial judge.

Considering all that occurred in the trial, he concluded, the prosecutor's comment did not amount to reversible error. In support of an assessment of justice in the trial as a whole rather than in specific irregularities, he cites the words of Wiley Rutledge in *Kotteakos v. United States:*

> [T]he question is . . . what effect the error had or reasonably may be taken to have had upon the jury's decision. The crucial thing is the impact of the thing done wrong on the minds of other men, not on one's own, in the total setting.
>
> This must take account of what the error meant to them, not singled out and standing alone, but in relation to all else that happened.[14]

It is a recurring theme.

Egregious Error

It may seem to belittle the distinction between trial and appellate functions for an appellate court to review the whole record rather than focus on specific error. But in fact review is not a search for as yet undiscovered faults or, certainly, for a fresh verdict, but an attempt to see whether justice was done, in the last analysis, despite possible faults. The review is guided by a rule of restraint that, after consideration of the entire record, the appellate court shall not impose its own judgment but ask whether the trial court, with its firsthand information, could have made the decision it did in the fair exercise of its discretion. Only if the error is egregious will it intervene. If the call is close, it defers.

Stevens makes the point in *Nixon v. Warner Communications, Inc.,* in which the majority, consisting of the four Nixon appointees and Potter Stewart, denied press requests for permission to copy White House tapes from the Watergate trial of Attorney General John Mitchell, presidential aides H. R. Haldeman and John Erlichman, and others, for possible broadcast or sale. Ste-

vens argues, in dissent, for deference to one of the two trial courts
that had considered the issue and to the court of appeals, which
had sided with the press.

> The question whether a trial judge has properly exer-
> cised his discretion in releasing copies of trial exhibits
> arises infrequently. It is essentially a question to be an-
> swered by reference to the circumstances of a particular
> case. Only an egregious abuse of discretion should merit
> reversal; and when the District Court and the Court of Ap-
> peals have concurred, the burden of justifying review by
> this court should be virtually insurmountable. Today's de-
> cision represents a dramatic departure from the practice
> appellate courts should observe with respect to a trial
> court's exercise of discretion concerning its own housekeep-
> ing practices.
> There is, of course, an important and legitimate public
> interest in protecting the dignity of the Presidency, and pe-
> titioner has a real interest in avoiding the harm associated
> with further publication of his taped conversations. These
> interests are largely eviscerated, however, by the fact that
> these trial exhibits are already entirely in the public do-
> main. Moreover, the normal presumption in favor of access
> is strongly reinforced by the special characteristics of this
> litigation. The conduct of the trial itself, as well as the con-
> duct disclosed by the evidence, is a subject of great histori-
> cal interest. Full understanding of this matter may affect
> the future operation of our institutions. The distinguished
> trial judge, who was intimately familiar with the ramifi-
> cations of this case and its place in history, surely struck
> the correct balance.[15]

Egregious error, in Stevens's view, is diagnosed pragmatically:
it is not the technical flaws in the proceeding that matter, typically, but their effect. The distinction is clearest in cases tried
before a jury, to whom legal technicalities may seem particularly
obscure or trifling. In *United States v. Greene,* he dissented from
the circuit court's affirmance of the conviction of a skyjacker, reasoning that the jury, without adequate instructions, may unlawfully have convicted a man innocent by reason of insanity in order
to guarantee his removal from society. The insanity defense was

unusually strong, and might be supposed to have led the jury to look upon the defendant as both insane and dangerous. Not understanding that federal law allows a court to confine an insane person for a period that may well be longer than the criminal sentence for the offense in question, the jury may have decided it had no choice but to protect society by finding a man guilty of a crime he did not have the capacity to commit.[16]

> If I am correct in my belief that a not guilty verdict entered in this case would not have been followed by the defendant's immediate release, quite clearly his defense was irretrievably prejudiced if the jury made such an assumption. . . .
> In my opinion, this case presents one of the rare situations in which the failure of the trial judge to give any advice at all to the jury on a matter that must have loomed large in their deliberations constituted plain error. It is almost inconceivable to me that if the jury had put to one side any concern about the consequences of a not guilty verdict, they would not have entertained a reasonable doubt as to the defendant's sanity. Since there is a substantial likelihood that the outcome of the jury's deliberation was affected by this omission, I would reverse and remand for a new trial. . . .[17]

He assumes that jurors, presented the choice, will favor common sense over legalism. They should be given enough information to make sound pragmatic judgments.

A comparable concern about the actual impact of a judge's words on jurors is seen in Stevens's dissent in *Lakeside v. Oregon.* A man tried for the crime of escape, for not having returned to prison at the expiration of an overnight pass, contended that he was not criminally responsible for his failure to return, because of "mental disease or defect." He chose not to testify on his own behalf, and at the conclusion of the trial, out of hearing of the jury, the judge announced his intention to include in his charge a standard instruction that the jurors not infer guilt from the defendant's silence. Defense counsel objected. "[T]hat's like waving a red flag in front of the jury," he said. The judge responded that he would give the instruction, as planned, for the defendant's own protection.[18]

Which would best serve the defendant's interests, the instruction or its omission? The Supreme Court ultimately held that a judge might give such an admonition over the defendant's objection.

> The petitioner's argument would require indulgence in two very doubtful assumptions: First, that the jurors have not noticed the defendant did not testify and will not, therefore, draw adverse inferences on their own; second, that the jurors will totally disregard the instruction, and affirmatively give weight to what they have been told not to consider at all.

Such assumptions, it concluded, are "speculative."[19]

Said Stevens, "For the judge or prosecutor to call it to the jury's attention has an undeniably adverse effect on the defendant. Even if jurors try faithfully to obey their instructions, the connection between silence and guilt is often too direct and too natural to be resisted. When the jurors have in fact overlooked it, telling them to ignore the defendant's silence is like telling them not to think of a white bear." He quotes Shakespeare ("for Brutus is an honourable man . . .") on the force of double meaning.[20]

> It is unrealistic to assume that instructions on the right to silence always have a benign effect. At times the instruction will make the defendant's silence costly indeed. . . . [T]he State must have a strong reason for ignoring the defendant's request that the instruction not be given. Remarkably, the Court fails to identify any reason for overriding the defendant's choice. Eliminating the instruction on request costs the State nothing, other than the advantage of calling attention to the defendant's silence. A defendant may waive his Fifth Amendment right to silence, and a judge who thinks his decision unwise may not overrule it. The defendant should also be able to waive, without leave of court, his lesser right to an instruction about his Fifth Amendment right to silence.[21]

It is defendant and counsel who are best able to make a decision about the probable effect of the judge's intended instructions.

In sum, Stevens is often willing to overlook a merely technical

error in a proceeding otherwise fairly conducted; but when decision making seems to have been fundamentally deranged—a jury
misled, for example—he votes to intercede even in the absence of
specific error.

Sometimes, however, it is the trial "as a whole" in which the
sheer number of errors is the basis of Stevens's disapproval. In
United States v. Barrett, for example, he dissented on this ground
from the circuit court's affirmance of the conviction of the county
clerk of Cook County, Illinois, for mail fraud, interstate travel in
aid of racketeering enterprises, and attempted tax evasion:

> In order to determine whether the cumulative effect of
> the several errors in the proceedings below was sufficiently
> prejudicial to require a new trial, it is necessary to evalu-
> ate their effect in the context of the entire record. It is not
> our function to determine guilt or innocence, but, rather,
> notwithstanding our own persuasion on the question of
> guilt, to determine whether the jury's judgment may have
> been substantially swayed by error.[22]

He describes errors, any one of which might well have been insubstantial by itself, which together in his judgment are serious
enough to require reversal: failure to take steps, such as continu-
ance of the trial, to counter the effects of unrestrained publicity
about corruption in local government; an imprudent quip by the
judge which might have linked the case at hand to another recently tried; the prosecutor's heavy reliance on a witness with a
financial interest in the case; the prejudicial joinder of separate
offenses; the erroneous exclusion of evidence supportive of the
defendant's theory of the case; inaccurate and prejudicial comments by the judge on testimony in court; and other remarks by
the judge, out of the hearing of the jury, which suggested he had
made up his mind about the defendant's guilt before all of the
evidence had been presented. Stevens concludes, with characteristic concern for consequences:

> This case brings to mind the trial of Titus Oates, a guilty
> man who was convicted by improper methods. Macaulay's
> observation about that trial is worth repeating: "That
> Oates was a bad man is not a sufficient excuse; for the
> guilty are almost always the first to suffer those hardships

which are afterwards used as precedents against the innocent."[23]

Many of these cases involve jury trials; but judges, too, can be
misled. In *United States v. Ott,* in which Stevens wrote for the
circuit court that a material misstatement to the trial judge was
prosecutorial misconduct requiring reversal, the prosecutor had
kept the judge from learning that an associate of the principal
government witness was an informer: "I will put on as many Government agents as I can that will say he was never an informant,
he never was."[24] Said Stevens, "We assume that . . . the trial attorney . . . did not know that his representation was factually erroneous. Nevertheless, when an unequivocal material representation of this kind is made to the trial judge for the purpose
of persuading him to make a ruling favorable to the government,
the prosecutor is charged with the knowledge of his associates."
Because "'[t]he staff lawyers in a prosecutor's office have the burden of "letting the left hand know what the right hand is doing"
or has done,'" said Stevens, "we must regard as deliberate the
prosecutor's misstatement, his offer to produce inaccurate testimony, and his failure to correct his own misrepresentation."[25]

Even during appeals, attorneys for the United States refused to
admit knowledge of the falsity of the statement until presented,
from the bench, with information to that effect from another case.
The government had deceived the judge and engaged in serious
misconduct. The error was consequential in two respects: in con-
tributing to a verdict against the defendant and, seemingly more
important to the court in this case, in setting an unacceptable
precedent of official misbehavior.

To summarize to this point: Stevens is typically willing to give
trial courts the benefit of the doubt. They are and should be the
primary guarantors of due process. Appellate courts, however,
must closely monitor trials for abuse of discretion, and intercede
when injustice has been done.

Deference to Administrators

On questions of fairness, Stevens defers to administrators as he
does to trial courts. The circumstances differ, but the underlying

logic is the same: since decisions are best and most fairly made by those familiar with the facts at firsthand, appellate courts should intervene infrequently, according to their special expertise. He would limit the due process courts require of administrators, such as notice and hearing, and limit judicial review after the administrative decisions have been made.

In the years before 1972, the Supreme Court developed a balancing test for administrative due process, abandoning the right-privilege distinction which had tended to allow purely discretionary decisions unchecked by the Due Process Clauses. What remained was a simple formula: the weightier the individual's interest in a decision, the more stringent the requirements of due process. "A procedural rule that may satisfy due process in one context may not necessarily satisfy procedural due process in every case. Thus, procedures adequate to determine a welfare claim may not suffice to try a felony charge," the Court said in 1971, unanimously upholding a person's claim not to be deprived of a driver's license without due process of law.[26] In prior years the license might have been classed as a privilege rather than a right and the claim turned aside.

In 1972, in *Morrissey v. Brewer,* however, a divided Supreme Court set out a new, two-step test of due process: "The question is not merely the 'weight' of the individual's interest, but whether the nature of the interest is one within the contemplation of the 'liberty or property' language of the Fourteenth Amendment. Once it is determined that due process applies, the question remains what process is due."[27] On the same day, in *Board of Regents v. Roth,* it again distinguished the steps ("to determine whether due process requirements apply in the first place, we must look not to the 'weight' but to the *nature* of the interest at stake") and went on to reject a due process claim entailing, in its judgment, neither "liberty" nor "property" within the meaning of the Due Process Clause: "No State shall . . . deprive any person of life, liberty, or property without due process of law. . . ." (The language of the Fifth Amendment, applying to the federal government, is essentially the same.) The Court held that Roth, an assistant professor of political science at Wisconsin State University-Oshkosh, whose one-year contract was not renewed, had suffered no deprivation of liberty or property. The university therefore was not constitutionally obligated to tell him why he would not be rehired.[28]

Stevens had advanced a dual argument in dissent one year earlier as a freshman member of the court of appeals in *Shirck v. Thomas,* a case involving the refusal to renew a high school teacher's contract at the end of her probationary period. He contended that due process is concerned with neither the substance nor the wisdom of such decisions: it applies only in the event of deprivation of liberty or property protected by the Fourteenth Amendment, a point he did not elaborate, and it is directed only at procedure, not substance. When the Supreme Court decided *Roth* and overturned *Shirck* in the light of *Roth,* Stevens's objections to his circuit's broad reading of due process (in *Roth* as well, which had come before other members of his court) were vindicated. The Court's logic and Stevens's were consistent, and from then on Stevens worked to weave the two lines of thought together. For example, when *Shirck* returned in 1973, and it was Stevens's welcome duty to write for the court, he drew attention to "the decisive distinction between procedure and substance" as well, citing his previous *Shirck* dissent.[29]

It is worth examining the Court's logic and Stevens's contributions in more detail. In *Roth,* liberty interests are defined by an enumeration of specific rights accorded in previous cases, including freedom from bodily restraint, the right to engage in any of the common occupations of life, the right to establish a home and raise children, and the right to protect one's reputation. "It stretches the concept too far," however, "to suggest that a person is deprived of 'liberty' when he simply is not rehired in one job but remains as free as before to seek another."[30] Property, too, "may take many forms," adds the Court. "To have a property interest in a benefit, a person clearly must have more than an abstract need or desire for it. He must have more than a unilateral expectation of it. He must, instead, have a legitimate claim of entitlement to it."[31] Roth lost his case because he had no property interest beyond the last day of his one-year contract.

Stevens's special contribution has been to supply a parallel rationale for concentrating on procedures and avoiding reconsideration of administrative decisions on the merits. In 1974 he criticized the old process of reaching the merits: "The claim that a person is entitled to 'substantive due process' means, as we understand the concept, that state action which deprives him of life, liberty, or property must have a rational basis—that is to say, the reason for the deprivation may not be so inadequate that the judiciary will characterize it as 'arbitrary.'"[32] This overblown view of due process, he later explained, does not even require proof of unlawful intent: simple negligence becomes a ground for challenging administrative decisions. Then in 1976, in a five-to-four decision in *Bishop v. Wood,* concerning the discharge of a police officer, Stevens wrote an opinion of the Court in which the majority's unwillingness to concern itself with the merits was dramatically presented. Substantively, what evidence the Supreme Court had was on the side of the officer.

> In our appraisal of petitioner's claim we must accept his version of the facts since the District Court granted summary judgment against him. His evidence established that he was a competent police officer; that he was respected by his peers; that he made more arrests than any officer on the force; that although he had been criticized for engaging in high-speed pursuits, he had promptly heeded such criticism; and that he had a reasonable explanation for his imperfect attendance at police training sessions. We must therefore assume that his discharge was a mistake and based on incorrect information.

Even so, the officer had no constitutional claim. Under state law, he held his position at the pleasure of his superior. Said Stevens, "The Due Process Clause of the Fourteenth Amendment is not a guarantee against incorrect or ill-advised . . . decisions."[33]

In Stevens's view, the court that asks whether administrative decisions are wrong, not wrongly made, is acting without principle. "[J]udicial fiat inevitably provides the measure of acceptable or unacceptable state action. It is this . . . version of substantive due process that has from time to time generated criticism that the federal judiciary is wont to arrogate to itself powers not granted by statute or by the federal Constitution." Why "fiat"? Because without substantive legal guidelines "other than the vague contours of the due process clause itself," judges resort to extralegal cues, including their own conceptions of good policy.[34]

> In final analysis the "due process" decision will not turn on any question of fair procedure but on a judge's evaluation of the substance of the administrative determination. I believe judges are qualified by experience and training to evaluate procedural fairness and to interpret and apply guidelines established by others; I do not believe they have any special competence to make the kind of policy judg-

ment that this case implicitly authorizes. The assumption
that they do invites the reaction that was produced by decisions such as Lochner v. New York.[35]

As he notes elsewhere, the meanings of "irrationality" and "arbi-
trariness" are so different from one year or court to another that
their use has brought serious criticism upon the judiciary. To him,
the concept of substantive due process is "an inscrutable sign-
post."[36]

(Stevens explicitly recognizes the legitimacy of one form of
"substantive due process" inquiry, however, involving "impermissible motivation," in which guidelines are adequate and decisions
by fiat unlikely: if a deprivation of the plaintiff's liberty or property seems due to racial, social, political, or religious discrimination, judicial review is appropriate.[37] He cites cases of the wrong-
ful removal of public employees:

> If it is accurate to characterize those decisions as sub-
> stantive due process cases, it should be noted that the con-
> cept affects the analysis of the property interest and the
> liberty interest in different ways. Thus, if an employee who
> has a property interest in his job is discharged for exercis-
> ing a constitutional right, such a reason is impermissible
> and therefore, the equivalent of no reason at all—he may
> then have been deprived of property without substantive
> due process. Alternatively, if attention is focused on his
> First Amendment rights, for example, and if he is dis-
> charged for speaking out on an issue of public importance,
> even without a property interest in his job, the discharge is
> tantamount to punishment, and therefore is a deprivation
> of an interest in liberty. Recognizing that some depriva-
> tions of liberty can be justified by reasons acceptable to the
> judiciary, the absence of an acceptable justification may be
> characterized as a denial of substantive due process.[38]

But these are only incidentally due process issues: they are really
questions of equality and free expression with due process implications. Stevens's willingness to deal with them is not inconsistent with his basic aversion to substantive due process in the ordinary sense.)

Substantive due process is objectionable for more than its

illogic: it threatens to bring more power, responsibility, and, of course, work to an already burdened federal judiciary as well. If substantive due process were a proper judicial concern, he argues, everyone affected by a governmental decision would have a right to judicial review, and the courts would be unable to conserve their resources for significant federal questions.[39]

> We must accept the harsh fact that numerous individual mistakes are inevitable in the day-to-day administration of our affairs. The United States Constitution cannot feasibly be construed to require federal judicial review for every such error. In the absence of any claim that the public employer was motivated by a desire to curtail or to penalize the exercise of an employee's constitutionally protected rights, we must presume that official action was regular and, if erroneous, can best be corrected in other ways.[40]

Overload has worsened with the burgeoning of Sec. 1983 litigation, deriving from the language of the Civil Rights Act of 1871. According to present law, "Every person who, under color of any statute, ordinance, regulation, custom, or usage, of any State or Territory or the District of Columbia, subjects, or causes to be subjected, any citizen of the United States or other person within the jurisdiction thereof to the deprivation of any rights, privileges, or immunities secured by the Constitution and laws, shall be liable to the party injured in an action at law, suit in equity, or other proper proceeding for redress."[41] As Stevens cautioned in 1975, there are many ways a state can harm its people, each a potential deprivation of liberty or property, one might argue, bringing due process and the civil rights remedies of 42 U.S.C. §1983 into play.[42] But to interpret due process so broadly would be to invite a surfeit of litigation. Dissenting in a later case, Stevens writes that "our ability to perform our primary responsibilities can only be undermined by enlarging our self-appointed role as supervisors of the administration of justice in the state judicial systems." His concern expressed in such cases is that "we will soon become so busy that we will either be unable to discharge our primary responsibilities effectively, or else be forced to make still another adjustment in the size of our staff in order to process cases effectively. We should focus our attention on methods of using our scarce resources wisely rather than laying another course of bricks in the building of a federal judicial bureaucracy."[43]

Stevens's rationale for a restricted view of due process is part fidelity to the text, part practicality. He finds constraint in the words of the Constitution:

> Although I by no means suggest that the Due Process Clause may be understood by simply reading it, it is nevertheless appropriate to consider its text. The language of the clause identifies three limitations on its coverage. First, the harm suffered by the plaintiff must be a deprivation of life, liberty or property; second, the deprivation must be effected by the State; and third, it must have occurred "without due process of law."[44]

But at least as important in his view that judges should save themselves for the limited number of decisions they can make authoritatively and effectively (and all that implies to a pragmatist about finding and using facts), leaving the rest to others, including administrators, who can better make substantive judgments.

This is the first step in an approach to administrative due process supported by Stevens as circuit judge and Supreme Court justice, namely, the threshold questions whether "liberty" or "property" interests and procedural rather than substantive problems are involved. Assuming a positive answer, the second step is deciding how much process is due in a given case. Step one, in the language of Chapter 2, is simple or definitional balancing: a case must satisfy the appropriate constitutional standard or it is finished. Step two is compound balancing, in which various governmental and individual interests are weighed to arrive at the proper degree of procedural formality.

How Much Process Is Due?

"[D]ue process," says Stevens, citing precedent, "is a flexible concept which takes account of the importance of the interests at stake. . . ."[45] Just how account is taken may be seen in his dissent in *Bell v. Wolfish*. The majority of six, in an opinion by William Rehnquist, rejected a number of complaints about the treatment of inmates in a federal custodial institution designed primarily for pretrial detainees: double-bunking in rooms designed for one person, a rule barring hard-cover books not mailed directly from publishers or bookstores, a rule against receiving packages of food or personal items, body-cavity searches of inmates after visits with people from outside the institution, a rule that detainees be outside their rooms during routine inspections, and so forth.[46]

Inability to pay for a bail bond is no excuse for subjecting a detainee to a felon's punishments and indignities, Stevens protested. "It is not always easy to determine whether a particular restraint serves the legitimate, regulatory goal of ensuring a detainee's presence at trial and his safety and security in the meantime, or the unlawful end of punishment." But courts must see that such a determination has been made. The majority, he argued, has reduced the constitutional rights of these inmates to the level of a mere equal protection prohibition against irrational classifications or cruel-and-unusual-punishment protection from barbaric treatment. Due process, which provides much broader control of official behavior, has been overlooked.[47]

In each instance, Stevens finds that the harmfulness of the rule outweighs its regulatory objective. "The enforcement of these rules," he says, ". . . is a clear affront to the dignity of the detainee as a human being."

> To prohibit detainees from receiving books or packages communicates to the detainee that he, his friends, and his family cannot be trusted. And in the process, it eliminates one of his few remaining contacts with the outside world. The practice of searching the detainee's private possessions in his absence, frequently without care, offends not only his privacy interest, but also his interest in "minimal dignity." Finally, the search of private body cavities has been found to engender "deep degradation" and "terror" in the inmates: the price of such searches is so high as to lead detainees to forgo visits with friends and family altogether.[48]

His opinion, in its detail, is an instructive example of the pragmatist's wide-ranging analysis of benefits and costs, including the consideration of consequences and of less costly alternative regulations.[49] (See Appendix.) The majority opinion, by contrast, is characterized by deference to administrative authority.

This and numerous other cases illustrate Stevens's conviction that due process interests are of greatly varied weight. As an example, we may recall the case of the teacher who alleged that he was fired, among other reasons, for his hairstyle. In Stevens's view, such an individual choice is a constitutionally protected liberty, but a very minor one, readily outweighed by valid societal interests.[50] On the question whether a father has a constitutional right to be present at childbirth, a case noted in Chapter 1:

> The birth of a child is an event of unequalled importance in the lives of most married couples. But deciding the question whether the child shall be born is of a different magnitude from deciding where, by whom, and by what method he or she shall be delivered. In its medical aspects, the obstetrical procedure is comparable to other serious hospital procedures. We are not persuaded that the married partners' special interest in their child gives them any greater right to determine the procedure to be followed at birth than that possessed by other individuals in need of extraordinary medical assistance.
>
> Plaintiffs do not contend that they have a right to have the husband present without the consent of the attending physician. Implicitly, therefore, they acknowledge that their asserted right is subordinate to the dictates of sound medical practice. Having implicitly admitted that individual doctors may find valid medical reasons for excluding the father in individual cases, they must equally recognize that hospitals may also assume that the number of cases in which exclusion is appropriate is sufficiently large to justify the development of facilities and procedures in which the presence of the husband would be objectionable.[51]

Thus, even though a constitutional liberty or property claim has been asserted successfully in step one, it may be found so insubstantial in step two that the governmental interest prevails without further ado.

Stevens discusses the issue at length in *United States ex rel. Miller v. Twomey,* a challenge of prison disciplinary procedures. Segregating a prisoner from the general prison population or tak-

ing away his "good time" credits, effectively postponing his release at least twenty-one months, is a deprivation of liberty in the
constitutional sense, says Stevens. No longer is an inmate to be
regarded by the law as a mere slave. Precedent requires he be
accorded due process before losing a liberty of any significance;
how much due process, however, depends on the relative weight
of individual and institutional interest. At times the state's interest in quick action will outweigh the inmate's interest in procedural regularity.[52] But:

> In cases involving major rule infractions for which the
> punishment is severe, after the immediate crisis is past,
> the relative importance of the inmate's interest in a fair
> evaluation of the facts increases and the state's interest in
> summary disposition lessens; indeed, in such cases, in the
> long run the state's interest in a just result is the same as
> the individual's. For in those cases neither the state nor
> the inmate has any valid interest in treating the innocent
> as though he were guilty.[53]

The upshot is that basic procedural guarantees must be respected: inmates must be given proper notice of charges, a chance
to explain, and a factual determination by someone other than
the person reporting a violation of the rules.[54] The safeguards are
considerably more stringent than anything required in a prison
crisis, but less elaborate than mandated by previous cases for parole revocation, which, of course, falls short of the procedural requirements for a criminal trial.

(In *Lassiter v. Department of Social Services,* on the question
whether a woman whose child is being taken by the state has a
right to free counsel, Stevens does say:

> In my opinion the reasons supporting the conclusion that
> the Due Process Clause of the Fourteenth Amendment en-
> titles the defendant in a criminal case to representation by
> counsel apply with equal force to a case of this kind. The
> issue is one of fundamental fairness, not of weighing the
> pecuniary costs against the societal benefit. Accordingly,
> even if the costs to the State were not relatively insignifi-
> cant but rather were just as great as the costs of providing
> prosecutors, judges, and defense counsel to ensure the fair-

ness of criminal proceedings, I would reach the same result in this category of cases. For the value of protecting our liberty from deprivation by the State without due process of law is priceless.[55]

But this is not a blanket rejection of balancing in due process cases, as the final sentence by itself might suggest. The right to counsel is a sine qua non of criminal due process and of non-criminal proceedings "of this kind." That leaves out a host of proceedings, however, in many of which the contrary interests would be more than pecuniary.)

There are two essential differences between "property" and "liberty" interests, according to Stevens. First, while liberty is a prior right based in natural law, property interests are created by ordinary positive law. This view of property may be seen in an opinion of the Supreme Court in 1972, while Stevens was a circuit judge: "Property interests, of course, are not created by the Constitution. Rather, they are created and their dimensions are defined by existing rules or understandings that stem from an independent source such as state law—rules or understandings that secure certain benefits and that support claims of entitlement to those benefits."[56] Stevens has given it his support in the years since as circuit judge and as justice of the Supreme Court. In 1974, concurring in a case about the removal of a state official by the governor, Stevens wrote:

The question whether Adams had a property interest in his position as a member of the Liquor Control Commission is, of course, purely a question of Illinois law. It is not for us to appraise the wisdom of the State's choice between giving such a Commissioner fixed tenure, on the one hand, or making his employment terminable at the unfettered discretion of the Governor, on the other. It is simply our job to identify the choice that Illinois has made, and to respect that decision. . . . [A]s a matter of Illinois law Adams could be removed whenever the Governor saw fit to recite the magic words, "incompetence, neglect of duty, or malfeasance in office." Adams was therefore not deprived of an interest in property within the meaning of the Fourteenth Amendment.[57]

In 1976, writing for the Supreme Court, he said, "A property interest in employment can, of course, be created by ordinance, or by an implied contract. In either case, however, the sufficiency of the claim of entitlement must be decided by reference to state law."[58]

By contrast, "liberty" is not defined by government, according to Stevens. In *Meachum v. Fano,* he says in dissent:

> The Court's holding today . . . appears to rest on a conception of "liberty" which I consider fundamentally incorrect.
>
> The court indicates that a "liberty interest" may have either of two sources. According to the Court, a liberty interest may "originate in the Constitution" or it may have "its roots in state law." Apart from those two possible origins, the Court is unable to find that a person has a constitutionally protected interest in liberty.
>
> If man were a creature of the State, the analysis would be correct. But neither the Bill of Rights nor the laws of sovereign States create the liberty which the Due Process Clause protects. The relevant constitutional provisions are limitations on the power of the sovereign to infringe on the liberty of the citizen. The relevant state laws either create property rights, or they curtail the freedom of the citizen who must live in an ordered society. Of course, law is essential to the exercise and enjoyment of individual liberty in a complex society. But it is not the source of liberty, and surely not the exclusive source.
>
> I had thought it self-evident that all men were endowed by their Creator with liberty as one of the cardinal unalienable rights. It is that basic freedom which the Due Process Clause protects, rather than the particular rights or privileges conferred by specific laws or regulations.[59]

A prisoner's rights are limited, but even so he retains a degree of liberty, at least a right to be treated with dignity, because of his humanity.[60]

Second, there is a difference in remedies for the defense of property and liberty interests, as he argues in a 1975 concurrence as a member of the court of appeals.

> Deprivations of liberty may require greater procedural safeguards than deprivations of property. Thus, for ex-

ample, the rule that an adequate hearing must precede the deprivation is subject to various exceptions when only property interests are at stake. The Supreme Court had repeatedly held in property cases that the demands of due process may be satisfied by an appropriate hearing and award of compensation after the initial deprivation has taken place. In property cases, the timing of the hearing is merely one factor affecting the fairness of the State's remedial process.[61]

He elaborates in dissent in *Ingraham v. Wright* on the Supreme Court two years later:

The constitutional prohibition of state deprivations of life, liberty, or property without due process of law does not, by its express language, require that a hearing be provided *before* any deprivation may occur. To be sure, the timing of the process may be a critical element in determining its adequacy—that is, in deciding what process is due in a particular context. Generally, adequate notice and a fair opportunity to be heard in advance of any deprivation of a constitutionally protected interest are essential. The Court has recognized, however, that the wording of the command that there shall be no deprivation "without" due process of law is consistent with the conclusion that a postdeprivation remedy is sometimes constitutionally sufficient.

When only an invasion of a property interest is involved, there is greater likelihood that a damages award will make a person completely whole than when an invasion of the individual's interest in freedom from bodily restraint and punishment has occurred. In the property context, therefore, frequently a postdeprivation state remedy may be all the process that the Fourteenth Amendment requires.[62]

In general, Stevens favors firm application of traditional principles of due process where personal liberty is most directly at stake, as in the criminal trial and sentencing process. Application is only a little less firm on certain questions of prison management and parole and of child custody. Property interests on the whole are less valued. In any given case, however, specific circumstances control. Note his concurrence in *Moore v. East Cleveland,* a case in which a closely divided Court voided a housing ordinance that, by defining "family" narrowly, prohibited two grandchildren who were cousins rather than siblings from living in their grandmother's house. Stevens saw the ordinance as an unconstitutional restriction of the grandmother's fundamental right to decide who might live on her property.[63] The other members of the majority chose to regard the ordinance as a restriction of liberty rather than property. If it is a property interest, clearly it is an important one. (*Moore* also illustrates the not uncommon difficulty of drawing a line between "liberty" and "property" in due process cases.)

Other due process questions have an importance for Stevens akin to crime and punishment because they impinge upon specific traditional rights. In an early civil tax case as circuit judge, he wrote that the writ of *no exeat republica,* in this instance to keep a taxpayer against whom the Internal Revenue Service was proceeding for taxes due from leaving the country with taxable assets, must be used sparingly because (citing precedent) "[t]his right to travel is 'a constitutional liberty closely related to rights of free speech and association. . . .' It cannot be abridged without due process of law." He found no reason to believe that the person in question would or could spirit assets out of the country and therefore denied the writ.[64] In the case of *Vance v. Terrazas,* where the right in question was citizenship, he said:

> In my judgment a person's interest in retaining his American citizenship is surely an aspect of "liberty" of which he cannot be deprived without due process of law. Because the interest at stake is comparable to that involved in *Addington v. Texas* [holding that a person's interest in the outcome of a civil commitment proceeding is of such weight that due process requires the state to justify confinement by clear and convincing proof rather than a mere preponderance of the evidence] . . . , I believe that due process requires that a clear and convincing standard of proof be met in this case as well before the deprivation may occur.[65]

Here the line between civil and criminal, as in certain cases between liberty and property, is not easily marked.

All in all, reviewing questions of trial or administrative performance, Stevens adheres to the standard he attributes to Wiley

Rutledge: "He believed in allowing wide discretion to judges, to juries, and to administrative agencies—always subject, however, to review for possible abuse."[66]

Conclusion

A parallel between the interpretation of statutes by trial judges and of musical scores by performers was once drawn by Jerome Frank: in each the extremes of slavish adherence to the text and free improvisation are less praiseworthy than a middle course of intelligent interpretation, faithful to the composer's or the legislators' intentions, but guided by more than text alone.[67] Frank's prescriptions are consistent with Stevens's view of the dual importance of principle and discretion in judicial decision making.

We can usefully extend the comparison to include appellate judging in the manner of John Paul Stevens. Appellate judges may be likened to music critics: both have middle courses to steer between self-restraint and activism, as do trial judges and musical performers. Beyond that, it is the appellate judge's goal to induce lower courts and administrators to act competently and fairly, as it is the critic's in the long run to encourage good playing—each without imposing merely personal judgments. Though moved, perhaps, by personal memories and preferences as erstwhile performers themselves, as reviewers they are also governed by norms of impersonality and neutrality. They judge quality in the light of widely recognized critical standards. (The standards are more closely defined for Beethoven and for trials, the classical performances of the law, than for jazz and most administrative decision making, in which improvisation is the rule, with little theme and much variation—in both of the latter, there is more deference to individual interpretation.)

Now let us suppose, at the expense of realism, that our music critics are barred from any performance they wish to review and must be content to stand outside, where they try to imagine what is going on from the faint sounds that filter outdoors from the concert hall. Our exiled critics, unable to catch the subtleties of performance and appropriately mindful of their limitations under the circumstances, will feel justified in writing bad reviews only for the grossest of offenses—a confusion of *andante* and *presto,* let us say, or a succession of wrong notes. The trial and hearing records upon which appellate judges make decisions, too, are shadowy approximations of live judicial and administrative performances. Because of their remoteness (not to mention crowded dockets and, with respect to many administrative judgments, their lack of expertise), appellate judges may choose, as Stevens does, not to judge harshly unless the performance has clearly gone awry.

4

Equal Protection of the Laws

Justice Stevens is even more restrained on questions of discrimination (typically arising in the states under the Equal Protection Clause of the Fourteenth Amendment and in federal jurisdiction under the Due Process Clause of the Fifth Amendment) than on questions of fair procedure under the two Due Process Clauses and other provisions of the Bill of Rights. Discrimination cases more often involve complex issues of social and political policy on which he is inclined to defer to the judgment of elected legislators and executives. When judicial intervention is appropriate, however, Stevens's distinctive contribution is straightforward compound balancing of individual rights against the societal interest in treating one group differently from another. The majority, instead, approaches different kinds of classifications with predetermined levels of tolerance or suspicion.

For some time the Court has taken the position that equal protection applies to legislative or administrative classifications strictly or laxly according to the nature of the groups involved. At one time it used two standards; more recently, three. The strictest judicial scrutiny is applied to racial and ethnic classifications: "[A]ll legal restrictions which curtail the civil rights of a single racial group are immediately suspect. This is not to say that all such restrictions are unconstitutional. It is to say that courts may subject them to the most rigid scrutiny. Pressing public necessity may sometimes justify the existence of such restrictions; racial antagonism never can."[1] When such a classification is questioned in court, the government bears a heavy burden of demonstrating its constitutionality. If a classification works against women, the Court applies a moderate degree of scrutiny instead: "[C]lassifications by gender must serve important governmental objectives and must be substantially related to achievement of those objectives."[2] The government's and the complainant's burdens of proof are more nearly equal in such cases and the difficulty of predicting outcomes correspondingly greater. Finally, when a classification involves groups which the Court feels deserve neither a high nor a moderate degree of special protection, the complainant bears the burden of proving the absence of a rational basis for the classification.[3]

Under this three-tier scheme, deciding which level of scrutiny is appropriate is at least as important as applying it to the facts at hand. To a group interested in molding basic constitutional policy, it is all-important.

Stevens rejects the three-tier test and its two-tier predecessor. "There is only one Equal Protection Clause," he says in *Craig v. Boren,* a sex discrimination case.

> It requires every State to govern impartially. It does not direct the courts to apply one standard of review in some cases and a different standard in other cases. Whatever criticism may be leveled at a judicial opinion in implying that there are at least three such standards applies with the same force to a double standard.
>
> I am inclined to believe that what has become known as the two-tiered analysis of equal protection claims does not describe a completely logical method of deciding cases, but rather is a method the Court has employed to explain decisions that actually apply a single standard in a reasonably consistent fashion. I also suspect that a careful explanation of the reasons motivating particular decisions may contribute more to an identification of that standard than an attempt to articulate it in all-encompassing terms.[4]

Characteristically, he would avoid substituting a complicated judge-made standard for the pristine language of the Constitution. The meaning of the clause, he believes, is most clearly seen in specific applications—again, a preference for compound balancing of a variety of circumstances case by case over the simple or definitional balancing favored by the majority. He further suggests that the practical difference between the Court's approach to equal protection and his is modest, and in *Craig v. Boren,* indeed, his opinion is a concurrence, not a dissent. How much difference is a question explored in this chapter.

Because of the inherent complexity of discrimination cases, involving social judgments and at a minimum the comparison of one group's treatment with another's, it is convenient to deal with the legal issue in pieces: the process of diagnosing and approving or disapproving official discrimination breaks down into five steps, representing the basic concerns of Stevens and, in varying degrees, of the Court majority. Stevens's approach is distinctive at each step. (For clarity, one set of terms will be employed in this chapter: to "discriminate" will mean to treat people differently, either lawfully or unlawfully; to "discriminate individiously" will signify unconstitutionality.)

At the first step, laws or other government decisions which discriminate between groups in so many words are distinguished from those that do not. Second, a law which is neutral on its face may yet be found to affect different groups differently in its administration. If discrimination in language or effect is discovered, the next step is to look for noninvidious justification which may save it. Despite such justification, however, a law may be unconstitutional if its impact is dramatically different from group to group. Finally, an otherwise acceptable law may be found defective because of inadequate matching of those the law was intended to affect and those actually affected.

In this chapter, John Paul Stevens's views are examined on each point in turn.

Explicit Discrimination

Stevens has staked out his own position in the initial step where diagnoses are made of discrimination in the very words of the law. Contrary to the majority view, for example, he has declared that rules regarding pregnancy are sex classifications as such. But he has also deferred to the majority in later cases. His opinions on the question are of interest substantively but also illustrative of his respect for precedent and his willingness to work with a majority with whom he differs, once he has made his own views known.

In 1976, in *General Electric Co. v. Gilbert,* the Court held that a corporate disability-benefits plan which omitted pregnancy-related disabilities was not in violation of Title VII of the Civil Rights Act of 1964, prohibiting discrimination against anyone "with respect to his compensation, terms, conditions, or privileges of employment, because of such individual's race, color, religion, sex, or national origin." The opinion cited *Geduldig v. Aiello,* decided in 1974, before Stevens joined the Court: "'While it is true that only women can become pregnant, it does not follow that every . . . classification concerning pregnancy is a sex-based classification. . . . Absent a showing that distinctions involving pregnancy are mere pretexts designed to effect an invidious discrimination against the members of one sex or the other, lawmakers are constitutionally free to include or exclude pregnancy from the coverage of legislation such as this on any reasonable basis, just as with respect to any other physical condition.'"[5] The Court found the constitutional logic of *Geduldig* applicable to the statutory question in the *Gilbert* case. It continued: "Pregnancy is, of course, confined to women, but it is in other ways significantly different from the typical covered disease or disability. The District Court found that it is not a 'disease' at all, and is often a voluntarily undertaken and desired condition. We do not therefore infer that the exclusion of pregnancy disability benefits from petitioner's plan is a simple pretext for discriminating against women." As in *Geduldig,* according to the Court, "'There is no risk from which men are protected and women are not. Likewise, there is no risk from which women are protected and men are not.'"[6] In dissent, Stevens argues that the constitutional holding in *Geduldig* does not control the statutory construction of the *Gilbert* case: what the Constitution does not forbid, a statute may. It is simply that "the rule at issue places the risk of absence caused by pregnancy in a class by itself. By definition, such a rule discriminates on account of sex; for it is the capacity to become pregnant which primarily differentiates the female from the male." He adds, in a footnote, "It is not accurate to describe the program [as the Court does] as dividing 'potential recipients into two groups—pregnant women and nonpregnant persons.' . . . The classification is between persons who face a risk of pregnancy and those who do not."[7]

The following year, in *Nashville Gas Co. v. Satty,* the Court considered the question whether the same act allowed a company to strip an employee of all accumulated job seniority and to deny her sick pay even though employees on leave with other nonoccupational disabilities suffered neither deprivation. All nine members agreed that company policy violated the law with respect to seniority but not with respect to sick pay; they divided, however, on the reasons for their judgment. Stevens, concurring in the judgment, offered his own rationale, in which he bows to precedent.

> The general problem is to decide when a company policy which attaches a special burden to the risk of absenteeism caused by pregnancy is a prima facie violation of the statutory prohibition against sex discrimination. The answer "always," which I had though quite plainly correct, is foreclosed by the Court's holding in *Gilbert.* The answer "never" would seem to be dictated by the Court's view that a discrimination against pregnancy is "not a gender-based discrimination at all." The Court has, however, made it clear that the correct answer is "sometimes." Even though a plan which frankly and unambiguously discriminates against pregnancy is "facially neutral," the Court will find it unlawful if it has a "discriminatory effect."[8]

He then suggests a simple test of this "discriminatory effect," namely, "whether the employer has a policy which adversely affects a woman beyond the term of her pregnancy leave."[9] It is a case of making the best of what is to him a bad rule. He prefers to clarify the Court's position on the seniority and sick-pay question than to disagree with it openly. It is a strategy of compromise that contrasts with, say, William Brennan's and Thurgood Marshall's consistent votes against any and all death sentences, in unrelenting opposition to the majority position that capital punishment as such is not cruel and unusual punishment.

Thus from 1976 to 1977 Stevens is seen shifting from dissent on pregnancy-related claims to reluctant, qualified support of the majority's negative position. In 1978 comes another unexpected turn, in his opinion of the Court in *Los Angeles Dept. of Water &*

Power v. Manhart, holding that a municipality which operates a
pension plan providing equal benefits for men and women but
requiring larger contributions from women is in violation of Title
VII of the Civil Rights Act.[10] It is an opinion explored more fully
later on, cited here only for its bearing on *Gilbert.* The Court in a
sense has come round to Stevens's equal-rights position in *Gilbert*
to the effect that a classification based on sex-related risk is a sex
classification per se, at least under Title VII. In *Gilbert* the risk
was of pregnancy, in *Manhart,* of a longer and therefore costlier
life for women than for men. In *Gilbert,* Stevens would have decided against the exclusion of pregnancy-related disability from a
benefit plan, and in *Manhart* he did decide against a longevity-
related penalty in a pension program. A price is paid, however: in
Manhart he discards the pragmatic concept of risk. In his opinion
of the Court he considers the actuarial argument for different
treatment of the pensions of women and men, but rejects it, because of Title VII's requirement of treatment of the "individual"
rather than the group, on the theory that actuarial data describe
group rather than individual characteristics.

Rather than overrule the majority opinion in *Gilbert* and adopt
the logic of his dissent, however, Stevens chooses to distinguish
Gilbert in his *Manhart* opinion on the ground that its classification "did not involve 'discrimination based upon gender as such.'"

> The two groups of potential recipients which that case con-
> cerned were pregnant women and nonpregnant persons.
> "'While the first group is exclusively female, the second
> includes members of both sexes'" [citing language from
> which he had dissented in *General Electric Co. v. Gilbert*].
> In contrast, each of the two groups of employees involved
> in this case is composed entirely and exclusively of mem-
> bers of the same sex. On its face, this plan discriminates on
> the basis of sex whereas the General Electric plan discrim-
> inated on the basis of a special physical disability.[11]

Stevens is taken to task by Harry Blackmun in a separate opinion: "The Court's distinction between the present case and *General Electric*—that the permitted classes there were 'pregnant
women and nonpregnant persons,' both female and male—seems
to me to be just too easy." ("It is of interest," he adds, "that Mr.
Justice Stevens, in his dissent in *General Electric,* strongly pro-

tested the very distinction he now must make for the Court.")
Blackmun's points are well taken.[12]

Stevens's line of reasoning has a number of possible explanations. First, his is an opinion of the Court and may to some degree be a collective expression of the several justices, including those in the *Gilbert* majority. Second, to the extent the opinion represents his own view, Stevens may have been trying not to offend others on the Court by repudiating their work of two years past: one does not hold a majority together with I-told-you-sos. Third, Stevens's *Manhart* opinion may be understood as a further example of his respect for precedent, in bowing to the opinion of the Court in *Gilbert* retroactively. Given a bit grudgingly in the *Nashville* case, his deference to precedent in *Manhart* is offered without hint of earlier differences.

In cases in which it is possible to diagnose sex discrimination against both males and females, either in the language of the law or its impact, Stevens typically votes against the equal protection claim. In an early opinion as circuit judge, in *Sprogis v. United Air Lines, Inc.,* involving an application of the Civil Rights Act of 1964 to private employment practices, he dissented from the majority view that a no-marriage rule for female flight attendants was discriminatory. Because only females could become United Air Lines flight attendants, with few exceptions, he found no discrimination.

> A simple test for identifying a prima facie case of discrimination because of sex is whether the evidence shows treatment of a person in a manner which but for that person's sex would be different.
>
> Under this test, plaintiff was not the victim of discrimination because of sex, whether we assume the relevant classification is all United employees or just flight cabin attendants, for she has not shown that if she were a member of the opposite sex she would have had any greater employment opportunities either as a "stewardess" or as a "non-stewardess."[13]

Stevens does not concern himself, as does the majority, with the question whether the no-marriage rule stems from "a stereotyped attitude toward females."[14] Characteristically, he is more interested in the context in which a rule operates than in the possibly questionable motives of its framers. The Court thinks of invidious discrimination as being treated *badly*. Stevens thinks of it as being treated *worse*. Both men and women can be treated badly; they cannot both be treated worse. (*Sprogis* is one of the cases that drew the fire of feminist witnesses in the Senate hearings on the confirmation of Stevens as a member of the Supreme Court in 1975. Nan Aaron, president of the Women's Legal Defense Fund, argued that his opinion in the case was based on "preconceived notions of women" rather than law; Bella Abzug, a member of the House of Representatives, made a similar point. Margaret Drachsler, speaking for the National Organization for Women, found Stevens expressly antagonistic to women's rights.[15] Under questioning by Senator Edward Kennedy, Stevens, clearly uncomfortable discussing judicial batting averages, nevertheless noted that he had in fact voted for and against claims of women's rights about equally.)[16]

In 1977, as a member of the Supreme Court, he wrote for the majority that a married female flight attendant, fired in 1968 under the United Air Lines policy voided in the *Sprogis* case and rehired in 1972 as a new employee without having made a timely complaint in the interim, had not been treated less favorably after 1972 than males hired between 1968 and 1972.

> Nothing . . . indicates that United's seniority system treats existing female employees differently from existing male employees, or that the failure to credit prior service differentiates in any way between prior service by males and prior service by females. Respondent has failed to allege that United's seniority system differentiates between similarly situated males and females on the basis of sex.[17]

Again, it is an argument based on context. Under constitutional or statutory rules against discrimination, it is not enough to consider whether members of a group have suffered: if nonmembers of the group in question are found to suffer similarly, there is no discrimination.

Along the same lines, Stevens once argued, in concurrence, that a provision of a workers' compensation law harmed males only, while the majority was content to strike it down for discriminating against both males and females.[18] (He considers invidious discrimination against males to be as unlawful as invidious discrimination against females and has not felt compelled, as has the majority at times, to characterize a law that ordinary people would see working against men as discrimination against females.)

Disproportionate Impact

If there is no overt discrimination in the language of the law (sometimes a debatable point, we have seen), the next question is whether the law discriminates in fact. For Stevens and other justices it is a matter of drawing the line between significant and insignificant disparities; and, just as he examines a regulation for discrimination against nonmembers of the group in question, so he watches for adverse impact on nonmembers of a neutrally worded regulation, too. Both the degree of disproportion and the member-nonmember issue are seen in *Personnel Administrator of Massachusetts v. Feeney.* The Court held that Massachusetts did not discriminate against women, in violation of the Equal Protection Clause, in allowing veterans, the great preponderance of whom are men, an absolute lifetime preference in obtaining state jobs. In a brief concurrence, Stevens cites the key fact, for him, "that the number of males disadvantaged by Massachusetts' veterans' preference (1,867,000) is sufficiently large—and sufficiently close to the number of disadvantaged females (2,954,000)—to refute the claim that the rule was intended to benefit males as a class over females as a class."[19]

Stevens's insistence that males as well as females be protected from invidious sex discrimination stems from a broader principle hammered home in an early opinion as circuit judge. Dissenting in a complex gerrymandering case, *Cousins v. City Council,* to which we shall necessarily return a number of times in this chapter, he declared that *all* groups are protected.

> As a matter of principle, invidious discrimination against Americans of Polish, German, or Italian ancestry is just as indefensible as discrimination against Americans of African ancestry. It seems equally clear that such discrimination against Catholics, Jews, Protestants or Mor-

mons is in the same category. Unquestionably the same rules must be applied to the classification of voters on grounds of national origin, ethnicity, or religion, as race. It can be demonstrated that political groups are also entitled to equal treatment. . . .

. . . [T]he motivation for the gerrymander is a function of the *political* strength of the group at which it is directed. That motivation is unaffected by the kind of characteristic—whether religious, economic, or ethnic—that gives the group political cohesion. . . .

. . . The constitutionality of a gerrymander depends not on the identity of the rival group which the arrangement is designed to disadvantage, but rather on whether its unfairness is appropriately characterized as "invidious."[20]

Similarly, in concurring in the judgment in *Mobile v. Bolden* in 1980, he asserts that the amendment applies to religious, ethnic, economic, and political groups as well as to racial minorities.[21] It is an activist position, but it is also only one step in a decision chain that on the whole is notably restrained. He would apply the Equal Protection Clause broadly, it is true, but he would apply it sparingly, as we shall see.

In the *Cousins* gerrymandering case, Stevens sets out his most distinctive theme in equal protection cases: a preference for objective over subjective evidence of intent or lack of intent to discriminate invidiously. Sometimes courts look for evidence of improper personal motivation, by individual legislators, he says. If the evidence is there, the statute is unconstitutional; if not, it may be saved.[22] But there is a better approach.

In my opinion, customary indicia of legislative intent provide an adequate basis for ascertaining the purpose that a law is intended to achieve. The formal proceedings of the legislature and its committees, the effect of the measure as evidenced by its text, the historical setting in which it was enacted, and the public acts and deeds of its sponsors and opponents, provide appropriate evidence of legislative purpose. . . .

Regardless of one's appraisal of the procedures employed by the City Council of the City of Chicago, it demeans the legislative process to inquire into private conversations between aldermen or to draw an invidious inference from the fact that members of the Council are "acutely aware" of the racial composition of changing areas of the City. Of course they are. Responsible legislators are expected by their constituents, black and white, rich and poor, to be informed about such matters. I therefore would wholly reject the kind of subjective motivation analysis which the parties and the district court apparently considered relevant in this case.[23]

Concurring in 1976 in *Washington v. Davis,* he repeats the theme, further contrasting the two kinds of evidence:

Frequently the most probative evidence of intent will be objective evidence of what actually happened rather than evidence describing the subjective state of mind of the actor. For normally the actor is presumed to have intended the natural consequences of his deeds. This is particularly true in the case of governmental action which is the product of compromise, of collective decisionmaking, and of mixed motivation. It is unrealistic, on the one hand, to require the victim of alleged discrimination to uncover the actual subjective intent of the decisionmaker or, conversely, to invalidate otherwise legitimate action simply because an improper motive affected the deliberation of a participant in the decisional process. A law conscripting clerics should not be invalidated because an atheist voted for it.[24]

Nor, for Stevens, would a showing of subjective good faith—in this case in affirmative action efforts by the Washington, D.C., police department—save a policy objectively found to have an invidiously discriminatory purpose.[25]

The next year, in a school desegregation case, Stevens wrote a one-sentence concurrence reiterating his concern: "With the caveat that the relevant finding of intent in a case of this kind necessarily depends primarily on objective evidence concerning the effect of the Board's action, rather than the subjective motivation of one or more members of the Board, I join the Court's opinion."[26] In *Mobile v. Bolden,* more recently, he says that "a proper test should focus on the objective effects of the political decision rather than the subjective motivation of the decisionmaker." The latter, he adds, would prove unmanageable. Selective condemnation of electoral plans "on the basis of the subjective motivation of some of their supporters," he says, quoting Frankfurter, "'would spawn endless litigation concerning the multi-member district systems now widely employed in this country' and would entangle the judiciary in a voracious [!] political thicket."[27] Further, he notes in a later case, it is bad law.

> Although that criterion is often regarded as a restraint on the exercise of judicial power, it may in fact provide judges with a tool for exercising power that otherwise would be confined to the legislature. My principal concern with the subjective-intent standard, however, is unrelated to the quantum of power it confers upon the judiciary. It is based on the quality of that power. For in the long run constitutional adjudication that is premised on a case-by-case appraisal of the subjective intent of local decisionmakers cannot possibly satisfy the requirement of impartial administration of the law that is embodied in the Equal Protection Clause of the Fourteenth Amendment.[28]

One result of his reliance on objective rather than subjective evidence of intent, as he understands those terms, is that Stevens is less likely than he otherwise would be to overturn an official decision on equal protection grounds.

Neutral Justification

The next step, after diagnosing discrimination in the language or the impact of a law, is to determine whether it has any neutral, noninvidious justification. Stevens's strong tendency over the years has been to accept the justifications proffered by other decision makers (not any and all, however; and even a valid neutral justification may be balanced against the gravity of a specific complaint of unequal treatment).

An early example is *Rose v. Bridgeport Brass Company,* in 1973, in which Stevens dissented in part, refusing to see invidious discrimination under the Civil Rights Act of 1964 in the adverse impact of company policy on women. He was satisfied that the company had noninvidious reasons for what it had done. It was another of the opinions cited in his confirmation hearing to suggest insensitivity to sex discrimination.[29]

Because of illness, Mary Jeanne Rose was granted a leave of absence from her job as a blanking-press operator in 1969. A year later, having obtained permission from the company doctor to do light work with lifting of no more than forty pounds, she sought reemployment. She was informed that there were no openings in the plant. At the same time the company laid off forty-seven low-seniority employees in the department where she had worked, filling vacancies with more senior people from other parts of the plant. At least two men with less seniority than Rose, however, were given jobs in her old department. During her absence the company had redefined her position of blanking-press operator to include the work previously done by both operators and helpers and had required an ability to lift eighty pounds, formerly a requirement of the helper's job alone. Rose complained, among other things, that the redefinition was a deliberate attempt to keep her and other women from acting as press operators. The number of women with such jobs had dropped in this period from "at least" twenty-three, as the record puts it, to zero—a figure later corrected to two.[30]

Stevens's view was that none of the work rules was unjustified. He cited objective evidence of the company's nondiscriminatory reasons for each of the rules questioned and concluded:

> There is no dispute about the fact that the operating changes did produce economies, the fact that physical strength is related to job performance, or the fact that there are relatively fewer females than males with the physical strength required for this particular job. I am therefore not persuaded that this record contains any evidence supporting an acceptable inference of sex discrimination.[31]

The opinion in full is of equal interest for substance and for fact-consciousness.

In *Washington v. Davis,* Stevens voted to uphold "Test 21," given to applicants for positions as police officers in the District of Columbia as a test of verbal ability, vocabulary, reading, and comprehension. The Court notes that four times as many blacks as whites fail the test.[32] Nevertheless, according to the Court, its use does not amount to invidious discrimination. Says Stevens, in concurrence:

> First, the test serves the neutral and legitimate purpose of requiring all applicants to meet a uniform minimum standard of literacy. Reading ability is manifestly relevant to the police function, there is no evidence that the required passing grade was set at an arbitrarily high level, and there is sufficient disparity among high schools and high school graduates to justify the use of a separate uniform test. Second, the same test is used throughout the federal service. The applicants for employment in the District of Columbia Police Department represent such a small fraction of the total number of persons who have taken the test that their experience is of minimal probative value in assessing the neutrality of the test itself. That evidence, without more, is not sufficient to overcome the presumption that a test which is this widely used by the Federal Government is in fact neutral in its effect as well as its "purpose" as that term is used in constitutional adjudication.[33]

In 1979, in *New York City Transit Authority v. Beazer*, another case of disproportionate impact, Stevens reached a similar conclusion, writing for the Court. The case involved a rule prohibiting the employment of narcotics users in the Transit Authority, a sizable proportion of whose people drive buses, operate subway cars, or handle high-voltage equipment. The drug at issue in this case, methadone, is considered a narcotic by the authority. Methadone, the Court explains, is used as a painkiller, for short-term detoxification of heroin addicts, and in long-range "methadone maintenance programs." Most of those in maintenance programs in New York City are black or Hispanic, as are more than four-fifths of authority employees referred to a medical consultant for suspected violation of its drug policy.[34] Stevens concedes, in the absence of better statistics, that a prima facie case of invidious discrimination might be made, but finds the drug policy to be a demonstrably job-related, impartial rule: "[T]he evidence relied upon by the District Court reveals that even among participants with more than 12 months' tenure in methadone maintenance programs, the incidence of drug and alcohol abuse may often approach and even exceed 25%. . . . [T]he District Court recognized that at least one-third of the persons receiving methadone treatment—and probably a good many more—would unquestionably be classified as unemployable." The conclusion: "Quite plainly, TA's Rule 11(b) was motivated by TA's interest in operating a safe and efficient transportation system rather than by any special animus against a specific group of persons."[35] (In this case, as in *Rose*, Stevens's evidence of intent is objective.)

His conclusions are similar in cases of explicit nonracial discrimination. In 1978, dissenting in the case of *Caban v. Mohammed*, Stevens finds neutral justification (a "rational relationship . . . to the stated purpose for which the classification is being made") for a law requiring the consent of the natural mother, but not of the natural father unless he has lawful custody, for the adoption of a child born out of wedlock.[36]

> Men and women are different, and the difference is relevant to the question whether the mother may be given the exclusive right to consent to the adoption of a child born out of wedlock. Because most adoptions involve newborn infants or very young children, it is appropriate at the outset to focus on the significance of the difference in such cases.
>
> Both parents are equally responsible for the conception of the child out of wedlock. [He considers exceptions in a footnote.] But from that point on through pregnancy and infancy, the differences between the male and the female have an important impact on the child's destiny. Only the mother carries the child; it is she who has the constitutional right to decide whether to bear it or not. In many cases, only the mother knows who sired the child, and it will often be within her power to withhold that fact, and even the fact of her pregnancy, from that person. If during pregnancy the mother should marry a different partner, the child will be legitimate when born, and the natural father may never even know that his "rights" have been affected. On the other hand, only if the natural mother agrees to marry the natural father during that period can

the latter's actions have a positive impact on the status of the child; if he instead should marry a different partner during that time, the only effect on the child is negative, for the likelihood of legitimacy will be lessened.

These differences continue at birth and immediately thereafter. During that period, the mother and child are together; the mother's identity is known with certainty. The father, on the other hand, may or may not be present; his identity may be unknown to the world and may even be uncertain to the mother. These natural differences between unmarried fathers and mothers make it probable that the mother, and not the father or both parents, will have custody of the newborn infant.

In short, it is virtually inevitable that from conception through infancy the mother will constantly be faced with decisions about how best to care for the child, whereas it is much less certain that the father will be confronted with comparable problems. There no doubt are cases in which the relationship of the parties at birth makes it appropriate for the State to give the father a voice of some sort in the adoption decision. But as a matter of equal protection analysis, it is perfectly obvious that at the time and immediately after a child is born out of wedlock, differences between men and women justify some differential treatment of the mother and father in the adoption process.[37]

The Court, by contrast, found that the pertinent section of the New York Domestic Relations Law treated unmarried parents differently according to their sex without substantial relation to any important state interest and thus violated the Equal Protection Clause.

Neutral justification is all the more likely to be found in areas of the law in which special deference is traditionally due the "political" branches. In *Mathews v. Diaz,* for example, Stevens wrote for the Court (and not necessarily, therefore, quite as he would have written for himself in a separate opinion) that Congress may deny certain Medicare benefits to aliens who have not been admitted for permanent residence and have not lived in this country continuously. It has broad authority over immigration and naturalization, and may treat aliens differently from citizens.[38] But:

The real question presented by this case is not whether discrimination between citizens and aliens is permissible; rather, it is whether the statutory discrimination *within* the class of aliens—allowing benefits to some aliens but not to others—is permissible. . . .

For reasons long recognized as valid, the responsibility for regulating the relationship between the United States and our alien visitors has been committed to the political branches of the Federal Government. Since decisions in these matters may implicate our relations with foreign powers, and since a wide variety of classifications must be defined in the light of changing political and economic circumstances, such decisions are frequently of a character more appropriate to either the Legislature or the Executive than to the Judiciary. This very case illustrates the need for flexibility in policy choices rather than the rigidity often characteristic of constitutional adjudication. . . . Any rule of constitutional law that would inhibit the flexibility of the political branches of government to respond to changing world conditions should be adopted only with the greatest caution. The reasons that preclude judicial review of political questions also dictate a narrow standard of review of decisions made by the Congress or the President in the area of immigration and naturalization.[39]

There are cases he would decide the other way, but they are infrequent.[40]

Thus Stevens tends to look for and find neutral justification for laws and regulations challenged as invidiously discriminatory and to vote to sustain them.

Legislative Districting

In districting cases, Stevens holds out the possibility of finding invidious discrimination *despite* a substantial degree of neutral justification. But since he requires that evidence of invidious discrimination in such cases be overwhelming, to outbalance the exculpatory evidence, in practice the neutral justification tends to prevail. In *Cousins,* Stevens realistically assumes that the purposes of legislators are constitutionally impure. One could hardly expect lawmakers to ignore the impact of districting on various groups of voters. A test grounded on such an expectation would either invalidate all districting efforts or else induce legislators to hide their districting decisions behind closed doors.[41] But it is unlikely that the legislators' purposes are entirely impure. "If the basic plan is designed to follow historic political boundaries, natural barriers, or reflects a consistent endeavor to achieve compactness to the extent allowed by the requirements of contiguity, and, of course, if the equal population requirement is met, rarely if ever could a plan be attacked as wholly irrational."[42]

How then, in such ambiguous circumstances, is a court to make a judgment about invidious discrimination? In districting cases, the approach of strict scrutiny, requiring the demonstration of a compelling state interest, will not work. "Rarely would a state have a sufficiently strong interest in a particular set of boundaries, as opposed to alternatives which could be suggested, to satisfy that test."[43] The solution is to strike only at flagrant, unambiguous gerrymandering, as in *Gomillion v. Lightfoot,* in which the Court in 1960 threw out a redrawing of the city limits of Tuskegee, Alabama, from a square into a smaller, "uncouth twenty-eight-sided figure" that excluded all but four or five black voters but none who were white. Obviously, said Felix Frankfurter for the Court, it was a violation of the Constitution.[44] *Gomillion* may be viewed as an exercise in activism or restraint, depending upon one's perspective. It is activist because in this case the Court for the first time clearly stated that the dilution of voting rights was a constitutional concern and provided a footing for the reapportionment revolution shortly thereafter. *Gomillion* is restrained, however, because it concerns obvious gerrymanders and says nothing about more run-of-the-mill ones. This is Stevens's reading of *Gomillion,* emphasizing the limited applicability of the ruling rather than its egalitarian implications: "[I]f inexplicable, grotesque shapes, reminiscent of *Gomillion,* or the Massachusetts shoestring, or the Illinois saddlebag, should emerge, and if the pattern should be explicable only by reference to a purpose to segregate or to disadvantage a definable group, the absence of a permissible basis for the classification could be established by proof."[45]

This is not to suggest that every gerrymander may be identified by mere inspection of configurations. Unquestionably at times unique shapes will be produced by the need to satisfy the requirement of equal numbers or some other legitimate factor. But if a highly improbable shape is inexplicable except by reference to an impermissible gerrymandering purpose, in my opinion a challenge to the classification as resting on a ground wholly irrelevant to the achievement of a valid state objective should be sustained. In sum, notwithstanding equality of numbers, and notwithstanding the particular reason why the classification of voters was impermissible, I would expect another case like *Gomillion* again to produce prompt and unanimous disapproval from the Supreme Court.[46]

Gomillion, he concludes, remains a protection against "flagrant" gerrymandering. In a subsequent opinion on the same facts, he describes *Gomillion* as a case in which "the outcome was compelled by facts which spoke—indeed, shouted—for themselves."[47] (In *Mobile v. Bolden,* Stevens says that the logic of *Gomillion* need not apply only to circumstances as egregious as the Tuskegee gerrymander, it is true, but his other comments on *Gomillion* point the other way.) In *Karcher v. Daggett,* Stevens characterizes a New Jersey congressional districting plan as "well deserving the kind of descriptive adjectives—'uncouth' and 'bizarre'—that have traditionally been used to describe acknowledged gerrymanders," but reaches his conclusion against the plan on other grounds.[48]

Stevens applies the narrow reading of *Gomillion* to more than the detection of gerrymanders. It is employed in his concurrences in *Washington v. Davis* and *Mobile v. Bolden* as a reminder of the kind of dramatic or uncouth disproportion *not* before the Court in those cases.[49]

Another important precedent for Stevens, to the same effect as *Gomillion,* is *Yick Wo v. Hopkins,* a century-old decision which struck down a California municipal ordinance requiring special permission to operate a commercial laundry in a building not made of brick or stone. Though a racially neutral fire-safety ordinance on its face, the ordinance had been applied solely against Chinese: more than a hundred and fifty had been arrested for carrying on business without special consent, but no steps were taken against similarly situated non-Chinese. Every Chinese who applied for special permission, but only one who was not Chinese, was turned down. Said the Court:

> [T]he cases present the ordinance in actual operation, and the facts shown establish an administration directed so exclusively against a particular class of persons as to warrant and require the conclusion, that, whatever may have been the intent of the ordinances as adopted, they are applied by the public authorities charged with their administration, and thus representing the State itself, with a mind so unequal and oppressive as to amount to a practical denial by the State of that equal protection of the laws which is secured . . . by the broad and benign provisions of the Fourteenth Amendment to the Constitution of the United States.[50]

Like *Gomillion,* this is a case with qualities of both activism and restraint. It does assert that a law or ordinance need not discriminate explicitly to run afoul of the Equal Protection Clause: it is enough that it be shown to have been administered with discriminatory purpose and effect. But it, too, voids disparate treatment by race so blatant that once the Court was prepared to accept objective evidence, as Stevens would call it, a finding of invidious discrimination was unavoidable. It was, like *Gomillion,* an easy case, decided without dissent. It supports judicial restraint if it is accepted as an admonition to limit the application of the Equal Protection Clause to easy cases. That is Stevens's tendency.

In 1980, in *Mobile v. Bolden,* Stevens found no constitutional fault with Mobile's at-large city commission elections, in which no black had been elected to office since the elections began in 1911. His opinion concurring in the judgment begins with a distinction between official action that inhibits an individual's right to vote and "must be tested by the strictest of constitutional standards" and that which "affects the political strength of various groups that compete for leadership in a democratically governed community." Since the evidence is that blacks register and vote freely in Mobile, the political system is one that has an adverse effect upon one racial group within the electorate while treating individuals equally. There is no constitutional right to proportional representation for minorities, however, and it follows that not every showing of disproportionate impact on a historically disadvantaged group requires a judicial remedy.[51]

> The standard for testing the acceptability of such a decision [to adopt or retain an electoral plan] must take into account the fact that the responsibility for drawing political boundaries is generally committed to the legislative process and that the process inevitably involves a series of compromises among different group interests. If the process is to work, it must reflect an awareness of group interests and it must tolerate some attempts to advantage or to disadvantage particular segments of the voting populace. Indeed, the same "group interest" may simultaneously support and oppose a particular boundary change. The standard cannot, therefore, be so strict that any evidence of a purpose to disadvantage a bloc of voters will justify a finding of "invidious discrimination"; otherwise, the facts of political life would deny legislatures the right to perform the districting function. Accordingly, a political decision that is supported by valid and articulable justifications cannot be invalid simply because some participants in the decisionmaking process were motivated by a purpose to disadvantage a minority group.
>
> The decision to retain the commission form of government in Mobile, Ala., is such a decision. I am persuaded that some support for its retention comes, directly or indirectly, from members of the white majority who are motivated by a desire to make it more difficult for members of the black minority to serve in positions of responsibility in city government. I deplore that motivation and wish that neither it nor any other irrational prejudice played any part in our political processes. But I do not believe otherwise legitimate political choices can be invalidated simply because an irrational or invidious purpose played some part in the decisionmaking process.[52]

He is content to note that Mobile's at-large electoral system is one of the more common in the nation and therefore enjoys neutral justification.[53] It would be another matter if results adverse to a minority stemmed from a novel electoral system. Mobile's, old and familiar, does not fall into the *Gomillion* category.

Stevens's basic tendency to find a rational basis for discrimination is a case of judicial restraint, clearly, but not of pure form. True, in *Cousins v. City Council* he cites *McGowan v. Maryland*, the purest of all:

> Although no precise formula has been developed, the Court has held that the Fourteenth Amendment permits the States a wide scope of discretion in enacting laws which affect some groups of citizens differently than others. The constitutional safeguard is offended only if the classification rests on grounds wholly irrelevant to the achievement of the State's objective. State legislatures are presumed to have acted within their constitutional power despite the fact that, in practice, their laws result in some inequality. A statutory discrimination will not be set aside if any state of facts reasonably may be conceived to justify it.[54]

But, as we have seen, there are districting cases in which a degree of neutral justification is overcome by striking evidence of invidious discrimination in the pattern of *Yick Wo* and *Gomillion*.

The final step in the process of resolving discrimination cases offers another opportunity to find a neutral justification insufficient. It, too, qualifies the pure restraint of *McGowan,* which is satisfied by a bare minimum of neutral justification.

Adequate Fit

Perfect justification is a one-to-one relationship of legitimate legislative means and ends: the law discriminates (explicitly or in practice) as the legislature intended, neither affecting those who should not be affected nor neglecting those who should. *Washington v. Davis* is a case in point. In Stevens's view, the literacy test for police recruits in the District of Columbia efficiently serves the end of securing capable officers by weeding out all who lack the minimum reading and writing ability needed for the job, eliminating none with that ability. The requirement, in other words, is neither under- nor overinclusive. At the other extreme, he concludes that a New York State rule requiring state police to be citizens is wholly unrelated to the end of trustworthiness.

[A] rule which disqualifies an entire class of persons from professional employment is doubly objectionable. It denies the State access to unique individual talent; it also denies opportunity to individuals on the basis of characteristics that the group is thought to possess.

The first objection poses a question of policy rather than constitutional law. The wisdom of a rule denying a law enforcement agency the services of Hercule Poirot or Sherlock Holmes is thus for New York, not this Court, to decide. But the second objection raises a question of a different kind and a satisfactory answer to this question is essential to the validity of the rule: What is the group characteristic that justifies the unfavorable treatment of an otherwise qualified individual simply because he is an alien?

No one suggests that aliens as a class lack the intelligence or the courage to serve the public as police officers. The disqualifying characteristic is apparently a foreign allegiance which raises a doubt concerning trustworthiness and loyalty so pervasive that a flat ban against the employment of any alien in any law enforcement position is thought to be justified. But if the integrity of aliens is suspect, why may not a State deny aliens the right to practice law? Are untrustworthy or disloyal lawyers more tolerable than untrustworthy or disloyal policemen? Or is the legal profession better able to detect such characteristics on an individual basis than is the police department? Unless the Court repudiates its holding in *In re Griffiths* [voiding a state ban on the practice of law by aliens], it must reject any conclusive presumption that aliens, as a class, are disloyal or untrustworthy.[55]

Usually, however, Stevens sees the law in question as neither perfectly matched nor perfectly mismatched with legislative purpose. Nor is perfection required by the Equal Protection Clause. Thus in an early criminal case before the court of appeals he said, "Every defendant does not have the constitutional right to be represented by Clarence Darrow. Perfect equality between indigents and nonindigents, or among members of the class of nonindigents itself, is impossible to achieve."[56] As a practical person, he tolerates a degree of mismatch in the design of legislative classifications. Two of his opinions of the Court describe this position in broad terms, and may reasonably be taken as an expression of personal views since they are consistent with his separate opinions elsewhere. The first upholds a disability provision of the Social Security law:

> The provision challenged in this case is part of a complex statutory scheme designed to administer a trust fund financed, in large part, by taxes levied on the wage earners who are the primary beneficiaries of the fund. The entitlement of any secondary beneficiary is predicated on his or her relationship to a contributing wage earner. If the statutory requirements for eligibility are met, the amount of the benefit is unrelated to the actual need of the beneficiary. The statute is designed to provide the wage earner and the dependent members of his family with protection against the hardship occasioned by his loss of earnings; it is not simply a welfare program generally benefiting needy persons.
>
> Nor has Congress made actual dependency on the wage earner either a sufficient or a necessary condition of eligibility in every case. Instead of requiring individualized proof on a case-by-case basis, Congress has elected to use simple criteria, such as age and marital status, to determine probable dependency. A child who is married or over 18 and neither disabled nor a student is denied benefits because Congress has assumed that such a child is not normally dependent on his parents. There is no question about the power of Congress to legislate on the basis of such factual assumptions. General rules are essential if a fund of this magnitude is to be administered with a modicum of efficiency, even though such rules inevitably produce seemingly arbitrary consequences in some individual cases.[57]

In the second case, involving the New York City Transit Authority drug rule described above, Stevens writes:

> At its simplest, the District Court's conclusion was that TA's rule is broader than necessary to exclude those meth-

adone users who are not actually qualified to work for TA. We may assume not only that this conclusion is correct but also that it is probably unwise for a large employer like TA to rely on a general rule instead of individualized consideration of every job applicant. But these assumptions concern matters of personnel policy that do not implicate the principle safeguarded by the Equal Protection Clause. As the District Court recognized, the special classification created by TA's rule serves the general objectives of safety and efficiency. Moreover, the exclusionary line challenged by respondents "is not one which is directed 'against' any individual or category of persons, but rather it represents a policy choice . . . made by that branch of government vested with the power to make such choices." Because it does not circumscribe a class of persons characterized by some unpopular trait or affiliation, it does not create or reflect any special likelihood of bias on the part of the ruling majority. Under these circumstances, it is of no constitutional significance that the degree of rationality is not as great with respect to certain ill-defined subparts of the classification as it is with respect to the classification as a whole.[58]

Similarly, in a dissenting opinion that same year, he writes, "The mere fact that an otherwise valid general classification appears arbitrary in an isolated case is not a sufficient reason for invalidating the entire rule. Nor, indeed, is it a sufficient reason for concluding that the application of a valid rule in a hard case constitutes a violation of equal protection principles. We cannot test the conformance of rules to the principle of equality simply by reference to exceptional cases." Nearly identical reasoning may be found in cases on voting rights, abortion rights, and taxation.[59]

If Stevens frequently asserts the right of government to pursue legitimate ends by means of rough generalization, in other cases he insists with equal force that official discretion to design classifications is not unlimited. Typically he decides against a classification that is not wholly irrational by demonstrating that the harm done by its overinclusiveness outweighs the benefit of its properly targeted effects. Sometimes, too, he raises a question of underinclusiveness: whether the classification fails to cover those who should be covered if the law's purpose is to be served.

In his dissent in *Mathews v. Lucas,* for example, Stevens argues against the constitutionality of a complex provision of the Social Security Act granting surviving child's benefits automatically to legitimate children, but to illegitimate children only upon a showing of any of certain facts presumed to be associated with dependency. The logic of the Court is set out in an opinion by Harry Blackmun.

> Drawing upon its own practical experience, Congress has tailored statutory classifications in accord with its calculations of the likelihood of actual support suggested by a narrow set of objective and apparently reasonable indicators. Our role is simply to determine whether Congress' assumptions are so inconsistent or insubstantial as not to be reasonably supportive of its conclusions that individualized factual inquiry in order to isolate each nondependent child in a given class of cases is unwarranted as an administrative exercise. In the end, the precise accuracy of Congress' calculations is not a matter of specialized judicial competence; and we have no basis to question their detail beyond the evident consistency and substantiality. We cannot say that these expectations are unfounded, or so indiscriminate as to render the statute's classifications baseless. We conclude, in short, that, in failing to extend any presumption of dependency to appellees and others like them, the Act does not impermissibly discriminate against them as compared with legitimate children or those illegitimate children who are statutorily deemed dependent.[60]

In this instance, however, Stevens finds the classification both overinclusive, because it conclusively presumes all legitimate children to be dependent, and underinclusive, because it conclusively excludes some illegitimates who in fact are dependent. The children in question were ineligible because their father had not been supporting them at the time of his death, though he had done so for many years before. The classification is objectionable "because it attaches greater weight to support at a particular moment in time than to support of several years' duration." He concludes:

> Whether the classification is expressed in terms of eligible classes or in terms of presumptions of dependency, the

fact remains that legitimacy, written acknowledgments, or state law make eligible many children who are no more likely to be "dependent" than are the children in appellees' situations. Yet in the name of "administrative convenience" the Court allows these survivors' benefits to be allocated on grounds which have only the most tenuous connection to the supposedly controlling factor—the child's dependency on his father.

I am persuaded that the classification which is sustained today in the name of "administrative convenience" is more probably the product of a tradition of thinking of illegitimates as less deserving persons than legitimates.[61]

In *Craig v. Boren,* he argues in concurrence that a state law allowing females to drink at eighteen and males at twenty-one, in the name of traffic safety, is both underinclusive ("to the extent it reflects any physical difference between males and females, it is actually perverse" because "males are generally heavier than females" and "thus have a greater capacity to consume alcohol without impairing their driving ability than do females") and overinclusive:

> The legislation imposes a restraint on 100% of the males in the class allegedly because about 2% of them have probably violated one or more laws relating to the consumption of alcoholic beverages. It is unlikely that this law will have a significant deterrent effect either on that 2% or on the law-abiding 98%. But even assuming some such slight benefit, it does not seem to me that an insult to all of the young men of the State can be justified by visiting the sins of the 2% on the 98%.[62]

Another lengthy analysis of this sort may be seen in *Zablocki v. Redhail,* on marriage rights.[63] Adequacy of fit is a frequent concern in Stevens's opinions.

Conclusion

Seven contributions of Justice Stevens to the dialogue on equal protection stand out. First, with respect to the diagnosis of the words of a law, regulation, or decision, he has at times found discrimination in pregnancy-related provisions where other members of the court have not. Second, in analyzing either text or impact, he contends that if members of a group and nonmembers alike appear to suffer invidious discrimination neither suffers in the constitutional sense. Third, Stevens discounts subjective evidence of the intent of legislators and other officials to discriminate invidiously. An occasional racist statement during debate on a measure is of considerably less concern to him than, say, a collective statement of purpose or a clearly discriminatory impact ("normally the actor is presumed to have intended the natural consequences of his deeds"). Fourth, when noninvidious justification is offered, he is inclined to accept it. Fifth, on political matters such as gerrymandering or at-large *versus* district elections, he is unusually deferential to legislative judgments, on the ground that they are likely to be constitutional in at least some respects, such as numerical equality, and must therefore be proven grossly unconstitutional in others to be overturned.

Each of these is an occasion for marked judicial restraint on questions of equal protection. Cases which survive Stevens's tests, however, are put to another which proves less permissive, his sixth contribution, namely, the question of fit. Here, displaying his tendency to collect and weigh facts and to assess the adequacy of others' decision making, he analyzes the costs and benefits of legislative means to public ends. His conclusion, depending as it does upon the unique qualities of each law in context, is difficult to predict. Of the nine nonunanimous cases of the Supreme Court considered above on adequacy of fit, Stevens favored the equal protection claim (or its due process counterpart in federal jurisdiction) in four. (Brennan, the good liberal, favored the claim in all nine, and Rehnquist, the good conservative, opposed it in all nine.)

Seventh, on the fundamental question whether the equal protection test should be applied uniformly to all disputes or more stringently to some categories of cases than to others, Stevens says, we have noted, "There is only one Equal Protection Clause."[64] He is critical of two- and three-tier analysis; and, indeed, analysis of the full range of his opinions is far more straightforward by decision stages, as in this chapter, than by separate consideration of cases involving race, sex, poverty, and other classifications.

Still, if he generally rejects wholesale, a priori balancing, he also exhibits different degrees of suspicion in different kinds of cases. To take a distinctive example, he clearly dislikes laws which treat illegitimates and legitimates differently.

> However irrational it may be to burden innocent children because their parents did not marry, illegitimates are nonetheless a traditionally disfavored class in our society. Because of that tradition of disfavor the Court should be especially vigilant in examining any classification which involves illegitimacy. For a traditional classification is more likely to be used without pausing to consider its justification than is a newly created classification. Habit, rather than analysis, makes it seem acceptable and natural to distinguish between male and female, alien and citizen, legitimate and illegitimate; for too much of our history there was the same inertia in distinguishing between black and white. But that sort of stereotyped reaction may have no rational relationship—other than pure prejudicial discrimination—to the stated purpose for which the classification is being made.[65]

Perhaps it is best to describe his position as not wholly different from the Court's, but simply more flexible, and to recall his statement in *Craig v. Boren* that two- or three-tier analysis "is a method the Court has employed to explain decisions that actually apply a single standard. . . ."[66]

5

The Search for Balance

John Paul Stevens willingly draws guidance from text and precedent, when guidance is there, and heeds legislators, administrators, and trial judges when they seem in a better position to make
judgments, particularly on close questions. He is eclectic and
open-minded, an openness most conspicuous in his tendency to
gather and weigh facts and to balance in order to do justice to the
complexity of each case before the Court. Balancing is a good focus, then, for an assessment of Stevens's decision making.

The Debate over Balancing

The traditional criticism of the balancing of individual rights
against other values is that, in the process, rights tend to suffer,
though why and how much are points on which critics differ. Some
defenders of human rights object to balancing as such, others emphasize specific abuses arising in practice, and still others, the
general and the particular together. The broad concern is usually
framed in absolutistic terms, the specific, within the framework
of compound balancing.

A powerful voice against the balancing of constitutional rights
has been that of Ronald Dworkin. In 1970, in an article entitled

"Taking Rights Seriously," later to become a chapter in a book of the same title, he argued the presence of rights—to freedom of speech, for example—so fundamental as to be considered beyond the reach of government. They are prior "moral" rights against government—natural rights, in other words—not to be outweighed in individual cases by the good of the community: not by peace and quiet in public places, for example, or the maintenance of an environment to suit the tastes of the majority. Even lawful repeal of an unpopular fundamental right in the Constitution is wrong by Dworkin's standard. He is willing to put a fundamental right in the balance only in the event of a clash with another fundamental right (one's right to speak versus another's right not to suffer defamation by a casual remark, for example) or a genuine emergency in which, perhaps, the need for military secrecy may override the freedom of the press.[1]

Exceptional circumstances apart, government decision makers are morally bound to treat fundamental rights differently from other interests. Balancing is acceptable in lesser decisions: ". . . normally it is a sufficient justification, even for an act that limits liberty, that the act is calculated to increase what the philosophers call general utility—that it is calculated to produce more over-all benefits than harm." But Dworkin rejects the balancing of the demands of society and fundamental rights, though he describes the procedure sympathetically:

> The course of the government is to steer to the middle, to balance the general good and personal rights, giving to each its due.
>   When the Government, or any of its branches, defines a right, it must bear in mind . . . the social cost of different proposals and make the necessary adjustments. It must not grant the same freedom to noisy demonstrators as it grants to calm political discussion, for example, because the former causes much more trouble than the latter.

It is a plausible approach, he says, widely approved in the legal community. But it fails to take rights seriously.[2]

A well-known attack on balancing in general, based on a literal reading of the Constitution rather than on prior rights, is Hugo Black's opinion in *Barenblatt v. United States* in 1959. According to Black, constitutional guarantees expressed absolutely are to be applied absolutely. In this case of contempt of Congress for refusal to answer questions before the House Un-American Activities Committee, the majority held that the government's interest in self-preservation outweighed Barenblatt's associational rights. Black was uncompromising in dissent: "I do not agree that laws directly abridging the First Amendment freedoms can be justified by a congressional or judicial balancing process." Though appropriate for a regulation affecting rights indirectly—a key exception—balancing was not to be used to test actions of the government aimed squarely at limiting speech and political persuasion.

> To apply the Court's balancing test under such circumstances is to read the First Amendment to say "Congress shall pass no law abridging freedom of speech, press, assembly and petition, unless Congress and the Supreme Court reach the joint conclusion that on balance the interest of the Government in stifling these freedoms is greater than the interest of the people in having them exercised."[3]

Kenneth Karst notes that Black was in truth less than absolutistic, since he believed not every expression merited full protection. "All judges balance competing interests in deciding constitutional questions—even those who most vigorously deny their willingness to do so." If while insisting upon protecting all speech a judge deprecates obscenity, fighting words, and "speech-plus" as something less than "speech" in the constitutional sense, Karst says, he is indeed balancing. Similarly, Alexander Meiklejohn once drew a much-debated line between speech and nonspeech distinguishing "public" speech on public issues and politics, which required absolute protection, from "private"—the rest—which did not.[4]

Reasoning from the systemic requirements of constitutional democracy, rather than from the text as such or from prior rights, John Hart Ely in 1980 in *Democracy and Distrust* advocated a participation-reinforcing role for the judiciary, in the spirit of Harlan Stone's *Carolene Products* footnote and many of the Warren Court's speech, press, and discrimination decisions.[5] By this standard, some speech is of fundamental importance and some, such as the false advertising of cancer cures, is not. Ely prefers the "unprotected messages" approach of *Brandenburg v. Ohio* (as he reads the case) and *Cohen v. California* (a less ambiguous example) for judicial policing of the democratic system, fully allowing expression not falling into one of a few narrow categories clearly designated in advance, such as "advocacy of the use of force or of law violation . . . where such advocacy is directed to inciting or producing imminent lawless action" or "fighting words," saving balancing for cases in which the evil the government wishes to prevent is independent of the message. The wearing of an antiwar armband is fully protected under this rationale, but the destruction of draft board records is not, because in the latter case the damage does not stem from the message.[6] This is "simple" or "definitional" balancing, akin to absolutism, described in Chapter 2.

Ely finds fault with compound balancing in practice as well. It tends to be "flabby" in times of crisis, from war to McCarthyism, he says, when the need for judicial protection is greatest. He is critical of the clear and present danger test because it allowed the imprisonment of Schenck, Abrams, and Debs, the defendants in cases in which the test was introduced. He deplores much of the balancing that has occurred since.[7]

At times Black, too, argued less abstractly, from unhappy experience with compound balancing. Knowing the limited appeal of his literalism, he added in his *Barenblatt* dissent that if balancing must be done it must be done honestly:

> [B]ut even assuming what I cannot assume, that some balancing is proper in this case, I feel that the Court after stating the test ignores it completely. At most it balances the right of the Government to preserve itself, against Barenblatt's right to refrain from revealing Communist affiliations. Such a balance, however, mistakes the factors to be weighed. . . . [I]t completely leaves out the real interest in Barenblatt's silence, the interest of the people as a whole in being able to join organizations, advocate causes, and make political "mistakes" without later being subjected to governmental penalties for having dared to think for themselves.

Balancing is a "mere play on words" if it does not deal with the fundamental values at stake in litigation.[8] (One who rejected Black's literal-absolutistic approach might still agree with his secondary position that balancing may be fatally biased in practice.)

Karst meets Black on this ground as well, with an explicit formula for compound balancing that is sensitive to an array of factors for weighing. One who follows his guidelines is unlikely to ignore fundamental values entirely. Thus Karst argues both the inevitability and—properly done, with adequate information—the propriety of balancing in rights cases.[9]

The main issues of the balancing debate are embodied in the opposing opinions of members of the Court in a recent pair of search and seizure cases, *United States v. Leon* and *Massachusetts v. Sheppard,* of particular interest, as we shall see, because the majority opinions have drawn the praises and criticism, respectively, of Frank Easterbrook, conservative judge of the United States Court of Appeals in Chicago, formerly of the University of Chicago Law School, and Laurence Tribe, liberal member of the Harvard law faculty, in a lively exchange in the *Harvard Law Review.*[10]

In the summer of 1981, police in California received a tip that large quantities of illegal drugs were being sold by two people known as Armando and Patsy at their house in Burbank. A watch was kept. The police learned from an automobile license check that the man was Armando Sanchez, once arrested for possession of marijuana. Later another man, driving a car registered to Ricardo Del Castillo, a person with a similar arrest record, was seen entering the house and leaving shortly after with a small paper sack. Castillo's probation records pointed police to one Alberto Leon, whose phone number Castillo had given as his employer's. Leon, too, had been arrested on drug charges and was alleged by an informant to be heavily involved in drug importation. Earlier, police in nearby Glendale had told the Burbank police that Leon was said to have a large supply of drugs at his home in Glendale. He now lived in Burbank.[11]

Officers watched a number of people, at least one with a drug record, enter Armando Sanchez's house and leave with small parcels. Related activities were noted at Leon's house and at a nearby condominium. The movement of cars was monitored. Sanchez was observed leaving by plane for Miami, and upon his return his luggage was searched and a small amount of marijuana found. On the basis of this and other information, an experienced and well-trained officer applied for and was issued a search warrant.

An abundance of drugs and other evidence was found in the building and cars, and indictments followed. The accused filed motions
to suppress the evidence for want of probable cause for a warrant,
which were granted, with exceptions based on standing. In 1984
the issue was considered by the Supreme Court, in the case of
United States v. Leon.[12]

In the companion case, *Massachusetts v. Sheppard,* the Court
reviewed a claim that evidence leading to a conviction was inad-
missible because of a defective warrant. After a murder investigation, Boston police had filled out a search warrant application
(which would become the warrant itself when signed by a judge)
and a supporting affidavit. The application, however, was on an
old form designed for drug cases, used only because a better form
could not be found in the police station or obtained from court on
a Sunday. The police had been careful to delete one of two refer-
ences to "controlled substance" on the application. They found a
judge willing to consider the application at home. He was shown
the form and deletion, searched his office for an appropriate form,
found none, made some corrections of his own, and signed. The
words "controlled substance" remained intact in one place on the
warrant. An ensuing search turned up evidence that led to indictment and conviction.[13]

The Supreme Court found the evidence admissible in both
cases. Justice White wrote the opinions of the Court (one a brief
addendum to the other), joined by Chief Justice Burger and Justices Blackmun (who wrote a limiting concurrence as well), Powell, Rehnquist, and O'Connor, over the dissent of Justice Brennan, who was joined by Justice Marshall. Stevens wrote an
opinion dissenting in *United States v. Leon* and concurring in the
judgment in *Massachusetts v. Sheppard.* Most of the justices were
in their accustomed positions to the right or the left of center, in
other words, while Justice Stevens voted idiosyncratically according to his tendency and supplied his own rationale.

White balances in the drug case. The problem is whether the
Fourth Amendment exclusionary rule bars the use of evidence
obtained by officers acting in reasonable reliance on a warrant
issued by a neutral magistrate but later found unsupported by
probable cause. The answer is in the weighing:

> To resolve this question, we must consider once again the
> tension between the sometimes competing goals of, on the

one hand, deterring official misconduct and removing inducements to unreasonable invasion of privacy and, on the other, establishing procedures under which criminal defendants are "acquitted or convicted on the basis of all the evidence which exposes the truth."[14]

White does not question the judgment below, denying probable cause. From beginning to end, the opinion of the Court is a simple balancing of the costs and benefits of a good-faith exception to the exclusionary rule. It is largely composed of intuitive truths about costs from previous opinions: that overapplication of the exclusionary rule impedes the truth-finding functions of judge and jury, sets guilty defendants free or results in reduced sentences as a result of plea bargaining, generates disrespect for law and the administration of justice, and so on. On the benefit side, White looks for deterrent effects on police, magistrates, and judges in situations resembling the case at hand and finds them speculative at best. He concludes that "the marginal or nonexistent benefits produced by suppressing evidence obtained in objectively reasonable reliance on a subsequently invalidated search warrant cannot justify the substantial costs of exclusion." If there are no benefits of any importance, it matters not that it has little negative impact on police and prosecution, because it is already too costly. (The opinion of the Court in *Sheppard* cites the general logic of *Leon*, adding with regard to the makeshift form that it was not unreasonable for the police to have relied on the judge's assurances that, with necessary corrections, the warrant was authoritative.)[15]

White's opinion was cited by Easterbrook, before his appointment to the federal bench, as a model of judicial logic. Easterbrook and Richard Posner, also a former Chicago (and Stanford) law professor now on the court of appeals, have written widely on the application of economic analysis to law, particularly to common economic problems such as torts, contracts, and the regulation of monopolies, but also to certain questions of individual constitutional rights that attorneys and judges typically do not see as economic.[16] Two of Easterbrook's points are that judges should be forward-looking, concerned about the creation of rules, rather than backward-looking toward the resolution of past disputes, and that to that end they should understand how people will respond to the incentives their decisions create. Judges seek "efficiency" by treating the legal system as a kind of market in which, as Posner puts it, "human satisfaction as measured by aggregate consumer willingness to pay for goods and services" is maximized. "This approach attempts to reconstruct the likely terms of a market transaction in circumstances where instead a forced exchange took place."[17] Easterbrook illustrates:

> Once, the Court viewed securities as a part of moral philosophy. It asked whether a business practice was right or wrong, and it viewed even this question from an ex post perspective. (A practice was more likely to seem "wrong" if you overlooked how people chose the risks they would take and how they obtained explicit or implicit compensation for accepting those risks.) Today the Court is more likely to ask whether a business practice increases or reduces the expected return to investors. The different perspective leads the Justices in new directions.

"The new perspective spills over from economic to constitutional issues," he adds. "Exclusionary rule cases, once addressed in terms of 'judicial integrity' or the moral standing of police, are today treated as occasions for the assessment of the marginal deterrent effects of excluding particular categories of evidence" (citing *Leon*), to the dismay, he adds, of critics on the Court and elsewhere "who emphasize the noninstrumental functions of the exclusionary rule."[18]

In dissent in *Leon* and *Sheppard*, Justice Brennan challenges both the appropriateness and the soundness of the majority's exercise in balancing very much as Black did in *Barenblatt*. It is inappropriate, he says, because the balance was struck once and for all by the framers of the Fourth Amendment—in favor of liberty and privacy, at the cost of some reliable and incriminating evidence that the government might otherwise present in court—and the issue may not now be reopened. The amendment was intended to prohibit certain ways of gathering information and evidence. As a result, some incriminating evidence goes undetected. It is not the exclusionary rule but the Constitution itself which imposes this cost, however. For Brennan, the exclusionary rule is "compelled" by the Fourth Amendment and, except for *Wolf v. Colorado* in 1949, was long understood by the Court to be so. From 1974 on, however, the Court has made use of a "misguided and unworkable" rationale of deterrence in place of the established doctrine.[19] "In my view," he says, "a doctrine that preserves intact the constitutional rights of the accused, and, at the same time, is sufficiently limited to permit society's legitimate and pressing interest in criminal law enforcement to be served should not be so recklessly discarded." The issue is one of principle and is not now to be put in the balance. His apposition of "expediency" and "liberty and privacy" is at most a rhetorical balance. He quotes Holmes: "'If the search and seizure are unlawful as invading personal rights secured by the Constitution those rights would be infringed yet further if the evidence were allowed to be used.'"[20]

But there is more, quite apart from the intent of the framers, in Brennan's view:

> In addition, the Court's decisions over the past decade have made plain that the entire enterprise of attempting to assess the benefits and costs of the exclusionary rule in various contexts is a virtually impossible task for the judiciary to perform honestly or accurately. Although the Court's language in those cases suggests that some specific empirical basis may support its analyses, the reality is that the Court's opinions represent inherently unstable compounds of intuition, hunches, and occasional pieces of partial and often inconclusive data.

The Court's decision rests, he says,

> . . . on the ground that the "costs" of adhering to the exclusionary rule in cases like those before us exceed the "benefits." But the language of deterrence and of cost/benefit analysis, if used indiscriminately, can have a narcotic effect. It creates an illusion of technical precision and ineluctability. It suggests that not only constitutional principle but also empirical data support the majority's result. When the Court's analysis is examined carefully, however, it is clear that we have not been treated to an honest assessment of the merits of the exclusionary rule, but have instead been drawn into a curious world where the "costs" of excluding illegally obtained evidence loom to exagger-

ated heights and where the "benefits" of such exclusion are made to disappear with a mere wave of the hand.

Then, though a literalist and absolutist at heart, far closer to Black than to White, Brennan probes the empirical literature in even more detail than the other opinion writers, but concludes that "The extent of this Court's fidelity to Fourth Amendment requirements . . . should not turn on such statistical uncertainties."[21]

Laurence Tribe, commenting on Easterbrook's "law and economics" analysis of *Leon* and *Sheppard,* is at one with Brennan. In Tribe's view, the Court in these two cases "simply took out its calculator and punched in the costs and benefits of enforcing the Fourth Amendment in the case at hand."

> On the credit side of the Court's ledger was the marginal increase in deterrence of future fourth amendment violations. On the debit side was the perverse spectacle of a "guilty" man walking away scot-free: an affront to the system of justice. In the calculus employed by the Court, and promoted by Professor Easterbrook, the highly emotional and visible, indeed almost palpable, "cost" of enforcing the fourth amendment easily exceeded the nebulous and elusive "benefit" of vindicating the Bill of Rights and avoiding judicial complicity in denying the "security" from "unreasonable searches and seizures" promised by the fourth amendment. The fourth amendment predictably could not "pay its way" on these terms. . . .
>
> An obvious problem with this approach, however, is that the exclusionary rule was established by the unanimous Court in *Weeks v. United States* on a basis bearing no resemblance to this sort of pseudoempirical cost-benefit analysis. The exclusion of illegally seized evidence was instead deemed compelled by a direct constitutional command thought by the *Weeks* Court to be implicit in the fourth amendment itself: that courts not enter judgments of conviction based upon government action that violated a defendant's right to be "secure" from "unreasonable searches and seizures." The *Leon* majority's calculus overlooks this theory because it can assimilate only marginal utilities

and cannot allow for the introduction of an awkwardly ir-
reducible procedural principle into its analysis.[22]

Tribe does not abjure all "forward looking" analysis of costs and
benefits, to be sure. Like both Brennan and Stevens, he considers
both principle and the likely effects of alternative judge-made
search-and-seizure rules on members of the legal system. But
Tribe's conclusion, unlike the Court's, is supportive of the Fourth
Amendment: he is concerned that this and other decisions will
weaken the exclusionary rule and lead to more illegal searches
unless, as seems unlikely, other deterrents take over.[23]

Tribe contends (and Easterbrook denies, as does Posner in more
general language) that the tendency of the Court's and Easterbrook's cost-benefit analysis is to promote the "efficient" resource
allocation of classical economics and social Darwinism, without
regard for "distributive justice, procedural fairness, and the irre-
ducible and sometimes inalienable values associated with personal rights and public goods." It is not that Tribe favors value-
free judging; on the contrary, he deems it impossible. But he does
favor candor: his own values are unabashedly liberal and, as his
use of the word "inalienable" suggests, grounded in the natural
rights tradition of Locke and Jefferson—and Dworkin. Easterbrook's are conservative, beneath a surface of technocratic neutrality. The cost-benefit approach in the abstract is neither left-
nor right-leaning, of course; in White's and Easterbrook's hands,
however, it weighs principle and fairness to litigants lightly and
greatly emphasizes the value of deterrence (which it finds lacking). In looking forward, it has the effect of discounting liberal
values, shifting concern from people whose rights were actually
invaded to those who might or might not suffer in the unknown
future. Says Tribe, "Being 'assigned' a right on efficiency grounds,
after an appraisal of the relevant cost curves," for "purely contin-
gent and essentially managerial" reasons, does not satisfy our
need for inherent rights as human beings.[24]

Dworkin in the most general terms, Black and Ely in discussing the First Amendment, and Brennan and Tribe in the context
of a pair of cases on the exclusionary rule, all manifest the liberal's fear that compound balancing threatens individual rights.
The words of White, Easterbrook, and Posner suggest the fear is
not baseless: balancing can readily be used by conservatives to

justify deference to authority by giving scant weight to rights and much to order, efficiency, and administrative convenience.

But theirs is not the only way to balance.

Stevens's Balancing in Perspective

Before looking at Stevens's balancing closely, let us fix its position against two backdrops: first, briefly, balancing as one of a number of ways Stevens decides cases; and second, in more detail, the relative liberalism or conservatism of his voting compared with that of the other members of the Court and with Tribe's liberal preferences in selected cases.

Balancing is Stevens's characteristic approach. But there are others, as his single separate opinion for *United States v. Leon* and *Massachusetts v. Sheppard* well illustrates. Stevens dissents in *Leon,* finding no probable cause for the drug search, and concurs in the judgment in *Sheppard* on the ground that the "controlled substance" warrant was lawful. In *Leon* he defers to the trial court and its traditional generous reading of the warrant clause of the Fourth Amendment; in *Sheppard* he concludes pragmatically that the error in question was more technical than real. Apart from the conclusion, however, his reasoning as a whole in these cases is different from White's or Brennan's. It is more complex (a critic might say more miscellaneous).[25] More than anything it resembles the eclecticism of Benjamin Cardozo, who in *The Nature of the Judicial Process* described good judging as finding a dispositive rule in the Constitution or a statute, if possible, then if necessary resorting to a decisive precedent—again, if possible. If there is no such precedent, "the serious business of the judge begins. He must then fashion the law for the litigants before him." The judge's task is a twofold one: "he must first extract from the precedents the underlying principle, the *ratio decidendi;* he must then determine the path or direction along which the principle is to move and develop, if it is not to wither and die." By the method of analogy, he extracts principle from precedent; but should a competing principle have substantial support in history, the customs of the community, social utility, or "some compelling sentiment of justice," the judge must "balance all his ingredients, his philosophy, his logic, his analogies, his history, his customs, his sense of right, and all the rest, and adding a little here and taking out a little there, must determine, as wisely as he can, which weight shall tip the scales." Says Cardozo, "If you ask how he is to know when one interest outweighs another, I can only answer that he must get his knowledge just as the legislator gets it, from experience and study and reflection; in brief, from life itself."[26]

Balancing is crucial, then, when conflicting values must be compromised, a more frequent occurrence at the level of the Supreme Court of the United States than in the state courts that were the focus of Cardozo's analysis. Yet Stevens, like Cardozo, finds ways to handle some cases directly without recourse to consideration of costs and benefits or to judicial plugging of the law's gaps. First, in his opinion for these two cases, he quotes the "plain language" of the amendment and faults the majority for reading it in a way that allows a search to be "unreasonable" and "reasonable" at the same time—one is reminded of his insistence that a regulation cannot simultaneously deny both men and women, as such, equal protection of the law. Second, in the drug case, he objects to the fashioning of a broad "newfangled" rule where a very narrow holding will do: "The Court seems determined to decide these cases on the broadest possible grounds; such determination is utterly at odds with the Court's traditional practice as well as any principled notion of judicial restraint." Third, in the case of the inappropriate form, he makes a commonsense appeal to the "manifest purpose" of the words "particularly describe the place to be searched and the persons or things to be seized" in the amendment, namely, the prevention of general searches, and finds no such danger in the error at hand, especially since Sheppard was not at home at the time of the search and therefore lacked the citizen's interest in checking the scope of the officer's authorization by examining the warrant at the door.[27] Fourth, he examines the likely consequences of majority holding: "Under the majority's new rule, even when the police know their warrant application is probably insufficient, they retain an incentive to submit it to a magistrate, on the chance that he may take the bait. No longer must they hesitate and seek additional evidence in doubtful cases." And fifth, he reasons by analogy from other search-and-seizure cases, in which good evidence is often excluded, he notes, for a variety of reasons such as attorney-client, priest-penitent, and state secret privilege. The route differs, but the conclusion, in the drug case at least, is similar to Brennan's: the balance was made by the amendment's framers, and he is "not disposed to set their command at naught." Says Stevens, "It is of course true that the exclusionary rule exerts a high price—the loss of probative evidence of guilt. But that price is one . . . the Fourth Amendment requires us to pay. . . ."[28] It is a simple rather than compound balance in this case, capping a battery of approaches to reckoning the present meaning of the Constitution. Compound balancing is only one of Stevens's approaches.

A second perspective is the position of Stevens on the Court, derived from two sets of data: his vote and the majority's in eleven cases selected by Tribe to illustrate balancing at its worst, in 1984, and then his vote and the other members' in all nonunanimous cases of individual rights handed down from March 1976 to July 1986 in which Stevens participated.

Tribe includes *Leon* and *Sheppard* among the Court's decisions shortchanging the "constitutive" dimension of constitutional decision making, namely, the affirmation and shaping of values defining our society as it is and as we would like it to be.[29] The other four are:

Lynch v. Donnelly (465 U.S. 668), upholding municipal sponsorship of a Christmas nativity scene;
Regan v. Wald (468 U.S. 222), upholding a Treasury regulation that effectively banned tourist travel to Cuba;
Block v. Rutherford (468 U.S. 576), holding that pretrial detainees have no right of physical contact with spouses and children and no right to be present during shakedown searches of their cells; and
Hudson v. Palmer (468 U.S. 517), holding that the Fourth Amendment does not apply to prison cells.

Stevens voted with the majority in *Massachusetts v. Sheppard* and *Regan v. Wald*. He voted against (and therefore with Tribe) in *United States v. Leon, Lynch v. Donnelly, Block v. Rutherford,* and *Hudson v. Palmer*.

The other group of cases in Tribe's list raises "distributional" or equal protection questions:[30]

Clark v. Community for Creative Non-Violence (468 U.S. 288), upholding a ban on sleeping in, but not on occupying, tents
near the White House to call attention to the homeless;

City Council v. Taxpayers for Vincent (466 U.S. 789), upholding a
ban on posting signs on public property;

Selective Service v. Minnesota Public Interest Research Group (468
U.S. 841), upholding the denial of government educational
aid to those who failed to register for the draft;

Allen v. Wright (468 U.S. 737), rejecting, on procedural grounds, a
claim that the government should deny tax exemption to
private schools that practice racial discrimination; and

New York v. Quarles (467 U.S. 649), allowing an exception to the
Miranda rules in the case of an urgent public-safety need
to find a weapon discarded by a suspect.

In this group, Stevens voted with the majority in all but *Allen v.
Wright* and *New York v. Quarles*. In the cases as a whole, he voted
with the majority five times, with Tribe, six. Of the other justices,
only Blackmun shifted from side to side as did Stevens: he voted
with the majority six times and against, five. Brennan and Marshall dissented consistently (Marshall not participating in one
case); Burger, O'Connor, Powell, Rehnquist, and White voted together in all eleven cases.

A better test of Stevens's position vis-à-vis the other justices on
such questions is, of course, to be found in a tabulation of the
votes of the entire membership of the Court during Stevens's tenure. The cases considered (1) were those in which Stevens participated, (2) were accepted for argument and decided on the merits,
(3) involved a substantial question of individual rights, and (4)
were nonunanimous.[31] They are divided into an earlier period
(1976–81 or October terms 1975 through 1980), when Potter
Stewart was on the Court, and a later one (1981–86 or October
terms 1981 through 1985), beginning with the arrival of Sandra
O'Connor, his replacement, and ending with the retirement of
Warren Burger. (As it turns out, this division provides a good basis for observing Stevens's relative shift to the left—better than
tracking year by year, with erratic results from the different mix
of cases before the Court from one year to another.)

First a summary: on a scale indicating the percentage of votes
in favor of individual liberties, 100 signifying perfect liberalism
and 0, perfect conservatism, Stevens is well to the liberal side,

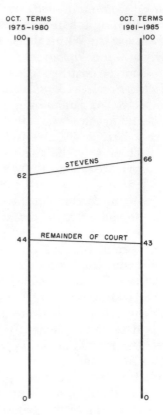

Fig. 1. Percent support for individual rights
in general by Stevens and remainder of
Court

and more so in recent years than before. The aggregate vote of
the other members of the Court was 44 percent for individual
rights during the first period and 43 percent during the second.
Stevens's votes were 62 percent for individual rights in the first
period, 66 percent in the second. Relatively, then, Stevens can be
said to have been substantially to the left of the rest of the Court
together for the first years, and even more so later on. (Strictly
speaking, that is all that can be said with confidence: the Court's
apparent ideological immobility may be that in fact, or an ideological shift in one direction offset by cases that on the whole, by
their facts, lean toward a decision in the other direction. Stevens's
shift, similarly, may be due to a change in thinking, a change in
cases, or both. But the relative positions of Stevens and the remainder of the Court—their distance from one another in each

period—are real.) On the basis of the figures, one might call Stevens a moderate in the first period, perhaps a moderate liberal in the second. At the very least, they indicate that a balancer need not be unfriendly to individual rights. The proof is in the results: the worst fears of Black, Dworkin, Ely, and Tribe are unrealistic with respect to *this* balancer, particularly in later years.

Stevens's move leftward, relative to the other justices, seems related to what he perceives as a crude jurisprudence of results on the right. Three pieces of evidence stand out. In 1984, dissenting from the summary disposition of a search and seizure case, *Florida v. Meyers* (see Appendix), he wrote:

> Since the beginning of the October 1981 Term, the Court has decided in summary fashion 19 cases, including this one, concerning the constitutional rights of persons accused or convicted of crimes. All 19 were decided on the petition of the warden or prosecutor, and in all he was successful in obtaining reversal of a decision upholding a claim of constitutional right. I am not saying that none of these cases should have been decided summarily. But I am saying that this pattern of results, and in particular the fact that in its last two and one-half Terms the Court has been unwilling in even a single criminal case to employ its discretionary power of summary disposition in order to uphold a claim of constitutional right, is quite striking. It may well be true that there have been times when the Court overused its power of summary disposition to protect the citizen against government overreaching. Nevertheless, the Court must be ever mindful of its primary role as protector of the citizen and not the warden or the prosecutor. The Framers surely feared the latter more than the former.[32]

No one who follows the Court would blink at a 19 to 0 pro-government score for Justice Rehnquist in any area of civil liberties, but in these cases it is the vote of a majority of the Court. Justice Stevens's exasperation is evident. Second, in the same year in a speech at Northwestern, he condemned the activist tendency of "members of the Court who are often described as 'conservatives'" to reach beyond the demands of the case at hand to lay down new and questionable doctrine. The third bit of evidence is the public debate on the meaning of the Constitution the following year between Stevens and Edwin Meese, attorney general, legal fundamentalist, and at the time front-runner for the next vacancy on the Court. Meese led off with criticism of the Court's broad interpretation of establishment of religion, its application of the First Amendment to the states, and in general its departure from the intent of the framers. Stevens's response, at a bar association gathering, was the first in living memory in which a sitting justice had criticized an attorney general by name. The statement is gentlemanly, but clearly suggests the intellectual poverty of the attorney general's law-and-order school of constitutional interpretation.[33]

For a justice who cares deeply about the quality of decision making, not to mention open-mindedness and moderation, the tendency of the Court toward assembly-line disposition of certain civil liberties cases in favor of government authority, illiberal overreaching, and the prospect of a new member with a dominant lifelong interest in law enforcement would be enough to induce a compensatory shift to the left.

The polarization of the Court is seen in the breakdown of the aggregate figures into individual voting tendencies. There are committed liberals, committed conservatives, a cluster of moderate conservatives, and Stevens well left of center. The greatest changes between periods, Blackmun's migration toward liberalism and the replacement of Stewart by the more conservative O'Connor, balance one another out. (For the record, the percentages of liberal votes on questions of individual rights in nonunanimous cases during the October 1986 term, Scalia having replaced Burger, are: Brennan, 96; Marshall, 93; Stevens, 71; Blackmun, 70; Powell, 32; O'Connor, 18; Scalia, 16; White, 14; and Rehnquist, 2. The figures might suggest increased polarization; but the number of such cases in one year is so small—56 in this term—that one should hesitate to draw any conclusions from them at all.)

Lastly, it is interesting to disaggregate Stevens's voting, and that of the remainder of the Court together for comparison, into major subject areas: speech and press, religion, due process (in the broad sense of the Fourteenth Amendment), and equal protection (including the use of due process in the Fifth Amendment to that end). Here, too, a cautionary statement is in order: even putting several years together, the number of First Amendment

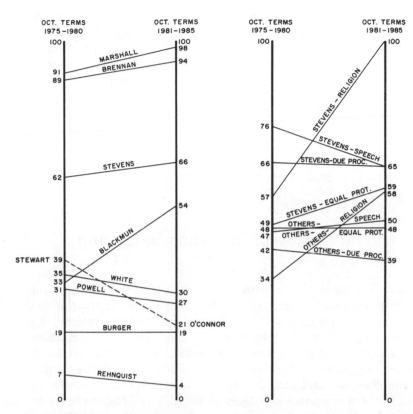

Fig. 2. Percent support for individual rights in general by members of Court

Fig. 3. Percent support for individual rights by major category, Stevens and remainder of Court

cases is small compared with those concerning due process and equal protection, and therefore one should be particularly wary of apparent shifts in ideological direction in the speech-press and religion categories. It is the ideological spread within periods that is most significant.

We can see that Stevens is more liberal than the rest of the Court in the aggregate on all four issues in both periods, except for equal protection in the first period. Second, Stevens prefers due process to equal protection, the other members on the whole the reverse. To put it another way, Stevens's voting on equal protection issues is not very different from that of the Court average, but on due process he is considerably more liberal. The most striking data are the liberal shifts by both Stevens and the Court on religious questions. There is no doubt, even allowing for the effects of too few cases and an increase in the proportion of establishment questions, that the lines depict a real shift to the left for both, which has come as no little surprise to Court watchers.[34]

In sum, while Stevens is not in the ideological camp of the leading critics of balancing, neither is he among the balancers they target for their strongest criticism. The voting patterns show why: when there is a clash of individual and authority, he favors the individual more often than not, and increasingly so.

The Nature of Stevens's Balancing

Fact gathering is Justice Stevens's way of discovering what is at stake in a case, an exercise in which "one's initial impression of a novel issue is frequently different from his final evaluation." It is exploration rather than first impressions, easy categorization, and simple balancing. The search for facts is wide-ranging. In varying degrees he investigates both "adjudicative facts" in the case at hand and "legislative facts," hard or speculative, about others in society similarly situated,[35] and thus in law-and-economics terms combines an *ex post* concern to settle the case fairly and *ex ante* intervention to affect the future (though not necessarily by adjusting incentives in Easterbrook's sense). The balancing that results is often compound: if he finds more than one value, they are weighed and balanced.

What he looks for is not facts for their own sake—we have noted his impatience with irrelevance—but facts, to repeat, that cast light on the stakes: Who gains? Loses? How? How much? In most cases two or more individual and societal values will appear to be affected retrospectively or prospectively by the Court's decision. In this pragmatic exercise, facts and values illuminate one another; particulars clarify generalities, and generalities, particulars. An openness to experience, in which sensitivity to facts and sensitivity to values are mutually reinforcing, is evident throughout Stevens's opinions. A typical example is his opinion of the Court in *FCC v. Pacifica Foundation,* noted in Chapter 2, upholding an administrative decision to accept and record a complaint against a radio station for broadcasting a monologue entitled "Filthy Words." Rather than deal with freedom of speech in the abstract, he notes a series of facts, each of which is related to basic personal or societal interests, and thus constitutional values, to be put in the balance. (1) It is a radio broadcast, which impinges on "the privacy of the home, where the individual's right to be left alone plainly outweighs the First Amendment rights of an intruder," not a book or a theater production. "Outside the home, the balance between the offensive speaker and the unwilling audience may sometimes tip in favor of the speaker, requiring the offended listener to turn away." (2) As such, it is also uniquely accessible to children, in whose well-being the government has a legitimate interest and over whom parents have a claim of authority. (3) It was heard by a young child (whose father complained to the Federal Communications Commission). Young children are more likely to be adversely affected than older children. The monologue was broadcast in the afternoon, when the very young are more likely to listen than at night. (4) Its plain language also affected its accessibility. For contrast, Stevens quotes a passage from the *Canterbury Tales* at least as lewd as anything in the monologue but relatively obscure and, of course, less likely to turn up uninvited in one's house. (5) That it was spoken rather than written made it available even to children who could not read. The "Fuck the Draft" message on a jacket worn in a public place, he notes, citing *Cohen v. California,* "might have been incomprehensible to a first grader," but this broadcast "could well have enlarged a child's vocabulary in a minute." (6) Further, the explicit language occurred in regular programming, not, for example, in a telecast of an Elizabethan comedy, to which a different audience would be tuned. (7) To support his view of the monologue as speech of relatively low constitutional value, he appends it in full (where it now sits, in law libraries and law offices across the country, safely inaccessible to all but callous adults and the most enterprising literate children). (8) Last, he deliberately does not decide that this broadcast would justify a criminal prosecution (in which other basic rights would be invoked).[36]

There are shadings of constitutional interest for the station, depending on medium, time of day, the nature of the programming of which the monologue was a part, and whether the government takes civil or criminal action, and for the listener, questions of place, as well, and of age. Stevens's distinctions, from the young child to the oldest—the preliterate, the literate and impression-able, and the literate and no longer quite so impressionable—have some of the form of Harry Blackmun's opinion of the Court in the leading abortion case, *Roe v. Wade,* assigning different in-terests in the first, second, and third trimesters of pregnancy, though the cases differ in scope, *Roe v. Wade* governing a full range of factual situations and Stevens's opinion in *FCC v. Paci-fica* not. *Pacifica* is a limited decision stemming from a similarly limited decision of the FCC concerning certain words in a certain context, Stevens notes repeatedly. And yet it weighs and balances several fundamental values: factual complexity begets value complexity. Paradoxically, then, particularizing is a means of dis-covering and invoking an array of relevant generalities, namely, values and their attendant principles; and the more the general-ities, the more bounded the decision as a whole.[37]

Stevens's "legislative" facts are commonsensical rather than statistical, by and large, more the common-law judge's qualitative review of the lessons of institutional and personal experience than the social-scientific data and generalizations of the legal realist. Stevens is not a quantitative empiricist on the order of the Blackmun of *Castenada v. Partida* or *Ballew v. Georgia* (nor does he have Blackmun's training in mathematics). There are nu-merous cases, it is true, such as *Craig v. Boren, Karcher v. Dag-gett,* and *Caban v. Mohammed,* described in Chapter 4, and *Rich-ardson v. Marsh,* noted in Chapter 1, indicating some willingness to use social-science information when occasion arises. And an openness to other kinds of facts is seen in his dissent in *California v. Carney,* a search and seizure case involving a motor home, which raised the question of the extent to which rules for motor vehicles or rules for houses should apply. Stevens referred to *Trailer Life, Motor Home,* and *R.V. Lifestyle Magazine* for an-swers. But, even so, he felt less than fully informed and said of the Court's opinion, "Rational decisionmaking strongly counsels against divining the uses and abuses of these vehicles in the vac-uum of the first case raising the question before us." Normally, however, his legislative facts are anecdotal and speculative—re-call, for example, his dissent in *Pennsylvania v. Mimms,* in which he hypothesizes realistically about the stakes for various kinds of drivers in various situations who might be asked by a police officer to step from a car, or his dissent in *H & H Tire Company v. United States Department of Transportation,* reviewing likely intended and unintended consequences of a federal regulation. In 1986, in *Goldman v. Weinberger,* Stevens voted against an air force officer's claim of a constitutional right to wear a yarmulke while in uniform. Though he saw grounds for a religious exemption from uniform dress regulations in this instance, Stevens also speculated that it would be worse for the military to decide future claims for exemptions not only on the basis of turbans and dreadlocks versus skullcaps but, as they inevitably would, according to the character and sincerity of religious faiths as well.[38]

When he balances, Stevens necessarily favors some values and slights others, just as Tribe, Easterbrook, and others do. There is always a thumb on the scales. As Tribe says, "Substantive perspective, reflecting the observer's past and context, is inescapable; its influence on perception and description is pervasive."[39] Still, on occasion, in a manner reminiscent of Hugo Black's secondary, pragmatic argument in *Barenblatt* and Tribe's comments on the reasoning of Byron White and Frank Easterbrook, Stevens is critical of blatant pro-government bias that allows efficiency to outweigh liberty.[40] A thumb, perhaps, but not the whole arm.

What distinguishes Stevens is not that he is neutral in his balancing, that he is either value free or scrupulously evenhanded, but that he is unusually sensitive to a diversity of values. Indeed, he has measurable value preferences: due process has an edge over equal protection, for example, in the pattern of his voting, and liberal values in general outweigh conservative. Still, there is no single concern as strong as, say, equality for Tribe. Stevens is willing to balance civil concerns against individual rights; he does not mechanically favor one over the other, as is the tendency of his more ideological associates on the left and the right. For Dworkin, behavior such as Stevens's amounts to not taking rights seriously. Dworkin makes a sharp distinction between individual rights and community values.[41] But Stevens's willingness to balance is not always a willingness to dilute fundamental rights to satisfy community preferences, though it is just that at times. It works in the other direction, too, in the assertion of fundamental individual rights where others see only a need for public order or convenience. His dogged insistence upon the rights of prisoners, because of their dignity as human beings, is a Dworkin-like sensitivity to fundamentals in the face of strong conventional arguments to the contrary. The same may be said of his First Amendment views on the *public* stake in prisoners' outgoing mail, on the right of the press to *gather* as well as print the news, and of public employees not to be fired because of party affiliation, or the concern that state aid might under some circumstances adversely affect church schools.[42]

Overall, the figures make clear, he enforces individual rights seriously but not rigidly. Nor does Tribe, for that matter, despite a far stronger commitment to liberal values: ". . . it is exactly when cases that trouble others *seem* easy from a given point of view that we should most deeply question how that point of view enables some to filter out so much to which we all ought to remain sensitive. . . ."[43]

In this spirit, Stevens decides by means of compound balancing. He is comfortable with "time, place, and manner" analysis in appropriate speech cases, for example, striking compromises between the rights of various speakers (those who can afford radio time or newspaper space versus those who cannot) and audiences (willing and captive).[44] The result in each case is a tailored decision, but by no means an abandonment of the First Amendment. Similarly, he is accustomed to exploring "fit" in equal protection cases, particularly the extent to which a legislative classification may be overinclusive, imposing costs on those caught in a broad statutory net, costs which outweigh the benefits of regulation.

His fact-bound approach will continue to displease liberals at times, and conservatives somewhat more often, because his concern for facts in all their complexity goes hand in hand with concern for values of equal complexity. More than the absolutist, Stevens is moved to explore, in order to learn what really lies behind and ahead of each case. It is an exercise in which Felix Frankfurter was a master.[45] But Frankfurter was far more likely than Stevens to wind up deferring to legislative authority. Of the two, therefore, it is Stevens who is the genuine balancer.

Other Moderates Compared

Much of Stevens's balancing, fact-consciousness, unconcern for ideology, and other pragmatic tendencies also are found in the work of the four moderates, broadly defined, with whom he has served: Potter Stewart (to 1981), Byron White, Harry Blackmun, and Lewis Powell (to 1987), all but White Republicans. All are eclectics, open to experience and distrustful of fixed rules; all render balanced, bounded judgments. All five are more or less unpredictable with respect to activism versus restraint and liberalism versus conservatism. It is a judicial role attributed by Gerald Gunther to John Marshall Harlan (1955–71), who

> . . . viewed balancing not as an escape from judicial responsibility, but as a mandate to perceive every . . . interest in a situation and to scrutinize every justification for a restriction of individual liberty. Moreover, after the closest possible analysis has isolated the crucial conflict of values, Justice Harlan strove for unifying principles that might guide future decisions. The Harlan legacy is devoid of simplistic rules and categorical answers; but it is rich in sensitive, candid, and articulate perceptions of competing concerns. . . .[46]

The differences among the five are shadings at most; many of the opinions of one could well have been written by another. Thus, as promised at the outset, this book is a reasonably representative case study of the Court's moderate center as well as a close analysis of Stevens's variations on moderate themes.

Substantively, in cases involving individual rights, each justice has a distinctive voting pattern. Stewart is most liberal on questions of speech, least on equal protection; White is relatively liberal on equal protection alone; from one period to the next Blackmun turns liberal, except in due process cases; Powell is fairly liberal with respect to speech and religion, conservative on questions of criminal due process and equal protection; and Stevens is relatively liberal across the board, particularly in the second period. Of the five, only Stevens takes a firm stand in favor of the rights of criminal defendants, among other things a reflection of his pervasive concern for fair and rational procedures. Stevens is the most self-consciously process-minded of the five. In general, he defers to legislators, administrators, and lower courts according to the quality of their decision making; in criminal cases, where life and liberty are at stake, he demands procedural regularity of the highest degree.

Distinctive patterns appear in the written opinions of the five, as in their votes. For all their similarities, they often disagree on rationale, even as they vote together. In *Richmond Newspapers, Inc. v. Virginia,* a First Amendment case, Stevens and Stewart wrote contrasting concurrences side by side and in *Fullilove v. Klutznick,* an equal protection case, dissents. In both cases, though it is a matter of degree, Stewart is the legalist, citing precedent at length, reasoning by analogy, and Stevens is the pragmatist.[47] Both show concern for facts and consequences but Stevens considerably more so—his emphasis is on how rules *work* rather than the weight of prior judicial opinion.

White is a balancer, as in *United States v. Leon.*[48] His balancing tends to be simple, however, as I have used the term, while Stevens's is characteristically compound. Within the same analytical framework, in other words, White's tendency is to generalize, to deal with an entire class of cases at one time; Stevens's is to particularize. The difference is evident in *New Jersey v. T.L.O.,* an application of the Fourth Amendment to the schoolhouse, for which White wrote the opinion of the Court and Stevens a separate opinion concurring in part and dissenting in part. White balances "the schoolchild's legitimate expectations of privacy" against "the school's equally legitimate need to maintain an environment in which learning can take place" and decides in a general way what is and is not appropriate in the school setting: neither a warrant nor probable cause is required for a search, for example. Stevens counters that the Court's ruling allows school administrators to search students suspected of the most trivial infractions. "For the Court, a search for curlers and sunglasses in order to enforce the school dress code is apparently just as important as a search for evidence of heroin addiction or violent gang activity." The weights instead should vary by circumstance; he would permit no invasion of students' privacy whatsoever in the enforcement of minor regulations. White's response is that the Court is "unwilling to adopt a standard under which the legality of a search is dependent upon a judge's evaluation of the relative importance of various school rules." Both balance, but one leans toward rules, the other toward facts. White is willing to particularize to the extent of recognizing that public schools are different from other institutions and require a specially tailored application of the Fourth Amendment; he will not go so far as to require further individualization by trial judges, case by case.[49]

Stevens and White squared off similarly a year later, in 1986, in an abortion case, *Thornburgh v. American College of Obstetrics and Gynecology,* in which Stevens concurs and White, objecting to the logic of *Roe v. Wade,* as he has from the start, dissents. White finds it illogical, for example, that *Roe* lends a fetus different weight in the constitutional balance at each stage of pregnancy. For White, the generalizer—again, relatively speaking, among the moderates—the governmental interest in protecting those "who will be citizens if their lives are not ended in the womb" does not change at the point of viability. For Stevens, the particularizer, that interest "increases progressively and dramatically as the organism's capacity to feel pain, to experience pleasure, to survive, and to react to its surroundings increases day by day. The development of a fetus—and pregnancy itself—are not static conditions, and the assertion that the government's interest is static simply ignores this reality."[50] As in *T.L.O.,* it is a question of fixed or variable weights, of simple or compound balancing.

Another difference between Stevens and White exhibited in *Thornburgh* is of degrees of interpretivism or noninterpretivism. From the interpretivist's perspective, of course, *Roe* is built out of thin air and is a proper litmus test of whether one does or does not take the words of the Constitution seriously. One of White's several arguments on the point in *Thornburgh* is that decisions based on constitutional "principles or values that cannot fairly be read into that document usurp the people's authority, for such decisions represent choices that the people have never made and that they cannot disavow through corrective legislation." Any constitutional right of sufficient force to overcome state legislation must be "fundamental" in some sense: "implicit in the concept of ordered liberty," "deeply rooted in this Nation's history"— traditional formulas which White finds inapplicable to abortion— or, best of all, based on the very words of the Constitution. "Fundamental liberties and interests are most clearly present when the Constitution provides specific textual recognition of their existence and importance."[51]

> When the Court ventures further and defines as "fundamental" liberties that are nowhere mentioned in the Constitution (or that are present only in the so-called "penumbras" of specifically enumerated rights), it must, of necessity, act with more caution, lest it open itself to the ac-

cusation that, in the name of identifying constitutional principles to which the people have consented in framing their Constitution, the Court has done nothing more than impose its own controversial choices of value upon the people.[52]

Stevens's view of constitutional liberty is more free-floating. He quotes Charles Fried approvingly: "What a person is, what he wants, the determination of his life plan, of his concept of the good, are the most intimate expressions of self-determination, and by asserting a person's responsibility for the results of this self-determinism we give substance to the concept of liberty." Says Stevens, "[I]t is far better to permit some individuals to make incorrect decisions than to deny all individuals the right to make decisions that have a profound effect upon their destiny."[53] Stevens is more open and speculative than White. White has more faith in rules than Stevens does.

In defense of his view that judges must judge, and not rely excessively on formulas, Stevens quotes an opinion of Justice Harlan, which White then cites *against* Stevens.

Due process has not been reduced to any formula; its content cannot be determined by reference to any code. The best that can be said is that through the course of this Court's decisions it has represented the balance which our Nation, built upon postulates of respect for the liberty of the individual, has struck between that liberty and the demands of organized society. If the supplying of content to this Constitutional concept has of necessity been a rational process, it certainly has not been one where judges have felt free to roam where unguided speculation might take them. The balance of which I speak is the balance struck by this country, having regard to what history teaches are the traditions from which it developed as well as the traditions from which it broke. That tradition is a living thing. A decision of this Court which radically departs from it could not long survive, while a decision which builds on what has survived is likely to be sound. No formula could serve as a substitute, in this area, for judgment and restraint.[54]

It is, says Stevens, an unsurpassed statement of "the difficult process of analysis and judgment that the guarantee of liberty requires." It is also a fair summary of the components of Stevens's own approach to judging, among them skepticism of simple rules, deference, moderation, and balance. White's reading of Harlan is very different: the balance in question is one "*struck by this country*," he insists, italicizing Harlan's words—"by the people themselves in constituting their system of government," adds White, not by judges imposing their own predilections.[55] For White the balancing occurred when the Constitution and the amendments were adopted; it is not the role of the Court to balance further. For our purposes it is of no particular concern that White has torn a phrase from context and given it a meaning entirely at odds with Harlan's; what is of interest is the strong interpretivist tendency of White, in contrast with Harlan and Stevens.

Justice Blackmun agrees with Stevens on many things, notably the importance of facts, context, and bounded decisions. Their differences are minor: Blackmun, like Stewart, is more formal than Stevens, less self-consciously methodological, and ambivalent about balancing, which Stevens employs openly and frequently. In *New Jersey v. T.L.O.*, for example, in which White engages in simple balancing and Stevens in compound balancing with respect to search and seizure, Blackmun warns that, though balancing such as White's may indeed be called for in cases such as this, it should not be regarded as a tool for general use. If Stevens is the particularizer and White the balancer-by-class, Blackmun is the reluctant balancer.[56] It is not that Blackmun will not balance—he *is* the author of *Roe v. Wade,* a fine example of balancing—but that he balances as a last resort.[57]

As the aggregate statistics indicate, the more liberal Blackmun of recent years differs substantially from Stevens only on criminal due process, among the categories tallied. Stevens leans to the liberal side in all; Blackmun, in all but one.

Our fourth fellow-moderate, Lewis Powell, gained a reputation as a generally conservative justice who nonetheless tended to vote with the liberals on key issues such as abortion and affirmative action. The press, in his later years and particularly in summing up at his retirement in 1987, often described him as the Court's swing vote. Powell demurred: he had not wished or tried to be that, he said, in the sense of withholding judgment until others had made their decisions.[58] But his indeed was a swing vote if it is defined simply as that of a moderate on a Court with wings but no solid majority, who in the process of voting as he saw fit made a conservative majority in some cases and a liberal majority in others. Whether he was *the* swing vote or simply *a* swing vote, and how he compares with Stevens, are other questions.

The clearest example of a swing vote in recent times is Blackmun's switch from the states'-rights side in *National League of Cities v. Usery* in 1976 to the nationalist side in *Garcia v. San Antonio Metropolitan Transit Authority* in 1985. In both cases the other members were evenly split; Blackmun's change of heart reversed the Court's position on application of federal minimum wage requirements to state and local governments. Powell is remembered for what has been termed his swing vote in *Regents of the University of California v. Bakke,* the vote of a moderate caught between liberal and conservative blocs of four. The outcome was not a vote swung to one side or another, in fact, but a compromise position that borrowed in part from one side and in part from the other. He was in a position to go one way or the other; he chose instead to straddle.[59]

More informative than such examples, perhaps, are the aggregate voting tendencies of Powell and other moderates, which can be drawn from the *Harvard Law Review*'s annual statistical compilation. From Stevens's first full term in 1976 through the 1985 term (the latest available at the time of my writing), for example, Powell was considerably more likely than Stevens to be in the majority—Stevens dissented more than twice as often as Powell. A sharper focus is available in the tabulations of 5-to-4 votes, which begin with the October 1981 term. These are the cases in which the opportunity to cast swing votes is greatest. Powell and White have been in the majority more often in these cases—101 and 100 times, respectively—than the other members of the Court; in Powell's case increasingly so in more recent years, Stevens, considerably less often—76 times. In these cases, it is Powell who has written the opinion of the Court most often, 2.7 times as often as Stevens. The data support the designation of Powell as *the* swing vote, in the sense of the uncommitted vote that makes the difference, with White not far behind, and Stevens's vote, equally uncommitted, less likely to swing the Court.

There are two apparent reasons for the greater tendency of Powell, compared with Stevens, to be on the winning side and, further, to be its spokesman: one is that the Court of late has tipped to the conservative side, facilitating the formation of a winning conservative coalition; but at least as important is Powell's ability to play the role of conciliator. In the retirement interview cited above, he said, "Whenever you're assigned to write a 5-to-4 decision, you know that you cannot afford to lose a vote. And sometimes you end up on the short end of a case when you start out with five votes, and that makes you more than a little unhappy."[60]

Stevens, by contrast, is more idiosyncratic, even contentious, preferring to express his own formulations than to build consensus. Again, the Harvard tabulations tell the story: in the period covering his first full term on the Court through the October 1985 term, Stevens wrote far more separate opinions (concurrences and dissents together) than any other justice. Powell, Stewart, and Blackmun each wrote a slightly greater number in one year (the 1977, 1978, and 1979 terms, respectively), but overall, Stevens is far ahead of the pack (395 separate opinions, compared with Powell's 242), and while Stevens's separate-opinion rate has been well ahead of everyone else's in the last six terms, Powell's declined after 1979. All of the moderates, then, are swing votes in the limited sense of casting votes on one side, then the other, case by case. But Powell and Stevens have demonstrated that within the role of swing vote there are degrees of influence and concern for consensus.

The differences among the moderates are indeed substantial. But, when the focus returns to their place in the Court as a whole, their similarities are evident.

Epilogue

John Paul Stevens's ways of judging differ from those of the doc-
trinaires of the left and right in two basic respects. The first is a
cluster of mutually reinforcing tendencies: particularizing, an appetite for adjudicative and legislative facts, sensitivity to disparate values, and compound balancing; the second, his strong procedural concern, particularly evident in an insistence that the
Court decide cases logically and clearly and that it defer to others
when they can do better because of their special skills or information. In both, Stevens exhibits a strong awareness of options:
of the substantive values embodied in facts and of the relative
merits of activist and restrained roles. He is pluralistic and eclectic, more the working judge of Cardozo's *Nature of the Judicial
Process* than ideologue or theorist.

Independent-minded pragmatists like John Paul Stevens are
unlikely to be appointed to the Supreme Court in any number in
the years ahead. It is an age of ideology again. Stevens is a free
spirit—a legal craftsman, but also a down-to-earth, case-by-case
arbiter of the strains and clashes of American society. By and
large, liberal presidents want predictable liberals on the Court,
and conservative presidents, predictable conservatives. Presidents almost always appoint members of their own party to the
Court.[1] Beyond that they quite understandably want justices who
will not oppose their programs. It is true that if they are wise in

the ways of the Court they know that justices do not bow down to presidents. Still, presidents hope for some ideological compatibility. If one of them faces a court laden with appointees of another persuasion, the temptation to shift the balance with safe appointees of his own will be all the greater.

Stevens was appointed under unusual circumstances. President Ford, in the wake of two bloody losing battles between Richard Nixon and the Senate over Supreme Court appointments (and a third narrowly averted by a strategic retreat), with a presidential election year approaching, could ill afford a partisan confrontation with a bruised, still-Democratic Senate and particularly not, as in the failed nominations of the Nixon years, a legal community outraged over mediocre selections. Ford's attorney general was Edward Levi, legal scholar and past law dean and president of the University of Chicago. Levi, with the help of Senator Charles Percy and the American Bar Association, was able to make a good recommendation, and Ford was in no position to reject it in favor of a more conventional political choice. In other times, with a weaker attorney general, a stronger president, and perhaps a Senate and president of the same party, it would be different.

It is not only presidents who favor policy-minded justices, however: scholars, too, often applaud justices who promote well-defined substantive values. One need only consider the reputation of John Marshall the nationalist or Earl Warren the equalitarian. Columbia law professor Vincent Blasi describes the Burger Court as comparatively weak at the extremes, left and right; but for the rest, "Seldom, if ever, in the Court's history has there been a period when the pivotal justices were as intelligent, open-minded, and dedicated as Potter Stewart, Byron White, Harry Blackmun, Lewis Powell, and John Paul Stevens." The problem from Blasi's point of view, however, is that the pivotal justices are "inspired not by a commitment to fundamental constitutional principles or noble political ideals, but rather by the belief that modest injections of logic and compassion by disinterested, sensible judges can serve as a counterforce to some of the excesses and irrationalities of contemporary governmental decision-making." It is a "centrist philosophy, dominant, transcending most ideological divisions, but essentially pragmatic in nature, lacking a central theme." It will not do. "The justices," Blasi concludes, "have crafted some significant practical compromises, but have not exerted any kind of moral force either by legitimizing nascent aspirations or by reinvigorating dormant ideals."[2]

One may accept Blasi's characterization of the moderates without agreeing that they lack moral force. If moral leadership is to labor single-mindedly for individual rights, or for the interests of the government, then Stevens and other moderates have failed. Stevens is complex—stodgy, perhaps—an incrementalist concerned with consensus and workability, who steers not by the stars but by familiar landmarks.[3] He is therefore profoundly conservative, in a procedural sense unrelated to Rehnquist's conservatism of results. He brings to mind William James's pragmatist for whom new ideas are grafted "upon the ancient stock with a minimum of disturbance of the latter. . . ." In his opinions the new idea "mediates between the stock and the new experience and runs them into one another most felicitously and expediently."[4] But I trust that anyone who digs into Stevens's judicial opinions will arrive at the conclusion that he is principled—sensitive, indeed, to more fundamental values than most members of the Court—and that he struggles to make the law clear and understandable. Of course he has "a commitment to fundamental constitutional principles," though perhaps not to "noble political ideals," if by that one means an agenda on the order of John Marshall's or Earl Warren's. He certainly lacks a central ideological theme.

Stevens offers a thoughtful alternative to central themes, liberal or conservative, written into the Constitution by one Supreme Court and set upon by another when old age and political winds have brought forth a new and different majority of justices. If nothing else, his work reaffirms an old conviction that there is deeper work to be done by the Court than the usual tug-of-war, depending more on numbers than on judgment, between the moral leaders of the right and the moral leaders of the left.

Appendix: A Stevens Sampler

In the first case, the Court upholds a set of rules for pretrial detainees in a federal detention center. Stevens dissents. An example of balancing with the balance tipped toward individual rights, of Stevens's disapproval of subjective evidence of intent, and of his tendency to defer to trial courts. *Bell v. Wolfish,* 441 U.S. 520, 583–86, 588–90, 592–95 (1979). Notes and citations omitted in this and following cases.

> The fact that an individual may be unable to pay for a bail bond . . . is an insufficient reason for subjecting him to indignities that would be appropriate punishment for convicted felons. Nor can he be subject on that basis to onerous restraints that might properly be considered regulatory with respect to particularly obstreperous or dangerous arrestees. An innocent man who has no propensity toward immediate violence, escape, or subversion may not be dumped into a pool of second-class citizens and subjected to restraints designed to regulate others who have. For him, such treatment amounts to punishment. And because the due process guarantee is individual and personal, it mandates that an innocent person be treated as an individual human being and be free of treatment which, as to him, is punishment.

It is not always easy to determine whether a particular restraint serves the legitimate, regulatory goal of ensuring a detainee's presence at trial and his safety and security in the meantime, or the unlawful end of punishment. But the courts have performed that task in the past, and can and should continue to perform it in the future. Having recognized the constitutional right to be free of punishment, the Court may not point to the difficulty of the task as a justification for confining the scope of the punishment concept so narrowly that it effectively abdicates to correction officials the judicial responsibility to enforce the guarantees of due process.

In addressing the constitutionality of the rules at issue in this case, the Court seems to say that as long as the correction officers are not motivated by "an expressed intent to punish" their wards, and as long as their rules are not "arbitrary or purposeless," these rules are an acceptable form of regulation and not punishment. Lest that test be too exacting, the Court abjectly defers to the prison administrator unless his conclusions are "'conclusively shown to be wrong.'"

Applying this test, the Court concludes that enforcement of the challenged restrictions does not constitute punishment because there is no showing of a subjective intent to punish and there is a rational basis for each of the challenged rules. In my view, the Court has reached an untenable conclusion because its test for punishment is unduly permissive.

The requirement that restraints have a rational basis provides an individual with virtually no protection against punishment. Any restriction that may reduce the cost of the facility's warehousing function could not be characterized as "arbitrary or purposeless" and could not be "conclusively shown" to have no reasonable relation to the Government's mission. This is true even of a restraint so severe that it might be cruel and unusual.

Nor does the Court's intent test ensure the individual the protection that the Constitution guarantees. For the Court seems to use the term "intent" to mean the subjective intent of the jail administrator. This emphasis can only "encourage hypocrisy and unconscious self-deception." While a subjective intent may provide a sufficient reason for finding that punishment has been inflicted, such an intent is clearly not a necessary nor even the most common element of a punitive sanction.

In short, a careful reading of the Court's opinion reveals that it has attenuated the detainee's constitutional protection against punishment into nothing more than a prohibition against irrational classifications or barbaric treatment. . . .

When measured against an objective standard, it is clear that the four rules discussed in Part III of the Court's opinion are punitive in character. All of these rules were designed to forestall the potential harm that might result from smuggling money, drugs, or weapons into the institution. Such items, it is feared, might be secreted in hard-cover books, packages of food or clothing, or body cavities. That fear provides the basis for a total prohibition on the receipt of hard-cover books (except from publishers, book clubs, or bookstores) or packages of food, for a visual search of body cavities after every visit, and for excluding the detainee from his cell while his personal belongings are searched by a guard.

There is no question that jail administrators have a legitimate interest in preventing smuggling. But it is equally clear that that interest is being served here in a way that punishes many if not all of the detainees.

The challenged practices concededly deprive detainees of fundamental rights and privileges of citizenship beyond simply the right to leave. The Court recognizes this premise, but it dismisses its significance by asserting that detainees may be subjected to the "'withdrawal or limitation'" of fundamental rights. I disagree. The withdrawal of rights is itself among the most basic punishments that society can exact, for such a withdrawal qualifies the subject's citizenship and violates his dignity. . . .

. . . The substantiality of the harm to the detainees cannot be doubted. . . . To prohibit detainees from receiving books or packages communicates to the detainee that he, his friends, and his family cannot be trusted. And in the process, it eliminates one of his few remaining contacts with the outside world. The practice of searching the detainee's private possessions in his absence, frequently without care, offends not only his privacy interest, but his interest in "minimal dignity." Finally, the search of private body cavities has been found to engender "deep degradation" and "terror" in the inmates; the price of such searches is so high as to lead detainees to forgo visits with friends and family altogether.

In contrast to these severe harms to the individual, the interests served by these rules appear insubstantial. As to the room searches, nothing more than the convenience of the corrections staff supports the refusal to allow detainees to observe at a reasonable distance. . . .

The prohibitions on receiving books and packages fare no better. The District Court found no record of "untoward experience" with respect to the book rule, and no support in the evidence for the petitioners' "dire predictions" as to packages. The simple fact is, as the record and the case law made clear, that in many prisons housing criminals convicted of serious crimes—where the inmates as a class may well be more dangerous, where smuggling is likely to be a far more serious problem, and where punishment is appropriate—packages of various sorts are routinely admitted subject to inspection. . . .

The body-cavity search—clearly the greatest personal indignity—may be the least justifiable measure of all. After every contact visit a body-cavity search is mandated by the rule. The District Court's finding that these searches have failed in practice to produce any demonstrable improvement in security is hardly surprising. Detainees and their visitors are in full view during all visits, and are fully clad. To insert contraband in one's private body cavities during such a visit would indeed be "an imposing challenge to nerves and agility". . . . Moreover, as the District Court explicitly found, less severe alternatives are available to ensure that contraband is not transferred during visits. . . .

It may well be, as the Court finds, that the rules at issue here were not adopted by administrators eager to punish those detained. . . . The rules can all be explained as the easiest way for administrators to ensure security in the jail. But the easiest course for jail officials is not always one that our Constitution allows them to take. If fundamental rights are withdrawn and severe harms are indiscriminately inflicted on detainees merely to secure minimal savings in time and effort for administrators, the guarantee of due process is violated.

In the next case, the Court approves the imposition of social security taxes on Old Order Amish over contentions that they provide their own welfare and are prohibited by their religion from both accepting public welfare and paying taxes in its support. Stevens concurs in the judgment. More compound balancing, this time in favor of the government. His underlying concern, however, is to guard against establishment of religion. *United States v. Lee*, 455 U.S. 252, 261–63 (1982). For a nearly identical concurring opinion on yarmulkes in the military, see *Goldman v. Weinberger*, 106 S.Ct. 1310, 1316 (1986).

The clash between appellee's religious obligation and his civic obligation is irreconcilable. He must violate either an Amish belief or a federal statute. According to the Court, the religious duty must prevail unless the government shows that enforcement of the civic duty "is essential to accomplish an overriding governmental interest." That formulation of the constitutional standard suggests that the Government always bears a heavy burden of justifying the application of neutral general laws to individual conscientious objectors. In my opinion it is the objector who must shoulder the burden of demonstrating that there is a unique reason for allowing him a special exemption from a valid law of general applicability.

Congress has already granted the Amish a limited exemption from social security taxes. As a matter of administration, it would be a relatively simple matter to extend the exemption to the taxes involved in this case. As a matter of fiscal policy, an enlarged exemption probably would benefit the social security system because the nonpayment of these taxes by the Amish would be more than offset by the elimination of their right to collect benefits. In view of the fact that the Amish have demonstrated their capacity to care for their own, the social cost of eliminating this

relatively small group of dedicated believers would be minimal. Thus, if we confine the analysis to the Government's
interest in rejecting the particular claim to an exemption
at stake in this case, the constitutional standard as formu-
lated by the Court has not been met.

The Court rejects the particular claim of this appellee,
not because it presents any special problems, but because
of the risk that a myriad of other claims would be too difficult to process. The Court overlooks the magnitude of this
risk because the Amish claim applies only to a small religious community with an established welfare system of its
own. Nevertheless, I agree with the Court's conclusion that
the difficulties associated with processing other claims to
tax exemption on religious grounds justify a rejection of
this claim. I believe, however, that this reasoning supports
the adoption of a different constitutional standard than the
Court purports to apply.

The Court's analysis supports a holding that there is virtually no room for a "constitutionally required exemption"
on religious grounds from a valid tax law that is entirely
neutral in its general application. Because I agree with
that holding, I concur in the judgment.

Stevens explains in a footnote:

In my opinion, the principal reason for adopting a strong
presumption against such claims is not a matter of administrative convenience. It is the overriding interest in keep-
ing the government—whether it be the legislature or the
courts—out of the business of evaluating the relative merits of differing religious claims. The risk that governmental approval of some and disapproval of others will be
perceived as favoring one religion over another is an important risk the Establishment Clause was designed to
preclude.

In *EEOC v. Wyoming,* the Court upholds the application to
state and local governments of a federal statute prohibiting age
discrimination. Stevens's concurrence sums up his views of American federalism, of the limits of *stare decisis,* and of judicial objectivity, 460 U.S. 226, 246–51 (1983).

[A]s the needs of dynamic and constantly expanding national economy have changed, this Court has construed the Commerce Clause to reflect the intent of the Framers of the Constitution—to confer a power on the National Government adequate to discharge its central mission. In this process the Court has repeatedly repudiated cases that had narrowly construed the Clause. The development of judicial doctrine has accommodated the transition from a purely local, to a regional, and ultimately to a national economy. Today, of course, our economy is merely a part of an international mechanism no single nation could possibly regulate.

In the statutes challenged in this case and in *National League of Cities v. Usery* (1976), Congress exercised its power to regulate the American labor market. There was a time when this Court would have denied that Congress had any such power, but that chapter in our judicial history has long been closed. Today, there should be universal agreement on the proposition that Congress has ample power to regulate the terms and conditions of employment throughout the economy. Because of the interdependence of the segments of the economy and the importance and magnitude of government employment, a comprehensive congressional policy to regulate the labor market may require coverage of both public and private sectors to be effective.

Congress may not, of course, transcend specific limitations on its exercise of the commerce power that are imposed by other provisions of the Constitution. But there is no limitation in the text of the Constitution that is even arguably applicable to this case. The only basis for questioning the federal statute at issue here is the pure judicial fiat found in this Court's opinion in *National League of Cities v. Usery.* Neither the Tenth Amendment, nor any other provision of the Constitution, affords any support for that judicially constructed limitation on the scope of the federal power granted to Congress by the Commerce Clause. . . . I think it so plain that *National League of Cities* not only was incorrectly decided, but also is inconsistent with the central purpose of the Constitution itself, that it is not entitled to the deference that the doctrine of *stare decisis* ordinarily commands for this Court's precedents. Notwithstanding my respect for that doctrine, I believe that the law would be well served by a prompt rejection of *National League of Cities'* modern embodiment of the spirit of the Articles of Confederation.

My conviction that Congress had ample power to enact this statute, as well as the statute at issue in *National League of Cities,* is unrelated to my views about the merits of either piece of legislation. As I intimated in my dissent in that case, I believe that federal regulation that enhances the minimum price of labor inevitably reduces the number of jobs available to people who are ready, willing, and able to engage in productive work—and thereby aggravates rather than ameliorates our unemployment problems. I also believe, contrary to the popular view, that the burdens imposed on the national economy by legislative prohibitions against mandatory retirement on account of age exceed the potential benefits. My personal views on such matters are, however, totally irrelevant to the judicial task I am obligated to perform. There is nothing novel about this point—it has been made repeatedly by more learned and more experienced judges. But it is important to emphasize this obvious limit on the proper exercise of power, one that is sometimes overlooked by those who criticise our work product.

The question in this case is purely one of constitutional power. In exercising its power to regulate the national market for the services of individuals—either by prescribing the minimum price for such services or by prohibiting employment discrimination on account of age—may Congress regulate both the public sector and the private sector of that market, or must it confine its regulation to the private sector? If the power is to be adequate to enable the National Government to perform its central mission, that question can have only one answer.

Stevens's dissent in *Florida v. Meyers,* 466 U.S. 380, 383–87 (1984), is an impassioned appeal for judicial restraint *and* individual rights.

No judicial system is perfect. In this case the Florida District Court . . . appears to have made an error. In the exercise of its discretion, the Florida Supreme Court elected not to correct that error. No reasons were given for its denial of review and since the record is not before us, we cannot know what discretionary factors may have prompted the Florida Supreme Court's decision. This Court, however, finds time to correct the apparent error committed by the intermediate appellate court, acting summarily without benefit of briefs on the merits or argument.

. . . Clearly, the law in this area is well-settled. That being the case, I see no reason why we cannot leave to the Florida Supreme Court the task of managing its own discretionary docket.

For three other reasons I believe the Court should deny certiorari in cases of this kind. First, our pronouncements concerning our confidence in the ability of the state judges to decide Fourth Amendment questions are given a hollow ring when we are found peering over their shoulders after every misreading of the Fourth Amendment. Second, our ability to perform our primary responsibilities can only be undermined by enlarging our self-appointed role as supervisors of the administration of justice in the state judicial systems. Dispositions such as that today can only encourage prosecutors to file in increasing numbers petitions for certiorari in relatively routine cases, and if we take it upon ourselves to review and correct every incorrect disposition of a federal question by every intermediate state appellate court, we will soon become so busy that we will either be unable to discharge our primary responsibilities effectively, or else be forced to make still another adjustment in the size of our staff in order to process cases effectively. We should focus our attention on methods of using our scarce resources wisely rather than laying another course of bricks in the building of a federal judicial bureaucracy.

Third, and perhaps most fundamental, this case and cases like it pose disturbing questions concerning the Court's conception of its role. Each such case, considered individually, may be regarded as a welcome step forward in the never ending war against crime. Such decisions are certain to receive widespread approbation, particularly by members of society who have been victimized by lawless conduct. But we must not forget that a central purpose of our written Constitution, and more specifically of its

unique creation of a life tenured federal judiciary, was to
ensure that certain rights are firmly secured *against* possible oppression by the Federal or State Governments. . . .
Yet the Court's recent history indicates that, at least with
respect to its summary dispositions, it has been primarily
concerned with vindicating the will of the majority and less
interested in its role as a protector of the individual's constitutional rights. Since the beginning of the October 1981
Term, the Court has decided in summary fashion 19 cases,
including this one, concerning the constitutional rights of
persons accused or convicted of crimes. All 19 were decided
on the petition of the warden or prosecutor, and in all he
was successful in obtaining reversal of a decision upholding a claim of constitutional right. I am not saying that
none of these cases should have been decided summarily.
But I am saying that this pattern of results, and in particular the fact that in its last two and one-half Terms the
Court has been unwilling in even a single criminal case to
employ its discretionary power of summary disposition in
order to uphold a claim of constitutional right, is quite
striking. It may well be true that there have been times
when the Court overused its power of summary disposition
to protect the citizen against government overreaching.
Nevertheless, the Court must be ever mindful of its primary role as the protector of the citizen and not the warden
or the prosecutor. The Framers surely feared the latter
more than the former.

In this case the Court upholds a limit of ten dollars on lawyers'
fees in connection with claims for veterans' benefits, against
the argument that the law passed during the Civil War has the
effect of denying veterans the right to assistance of counsel today.
Stevens dissents. *Walters v. Nat. Assn. of Radiation Survivors,*
473 U.S. 305, 358–59, 362–63, 365, 368–70, 371–72 (1985). Compound balancing.

The Court does not appreciate the value of individual
liberty. It may well be true that in the vast majority of
cases a veteran does not need to employ a lawyer, and that
the system of processing veterans benefit claims, by and
large, functions fairly and effectively without the partici-

pation of retained counsel. Everyone agrees, however, that there are at least some complicated cases in which the services of a lawyer would be useful to the veteran and, indeed, would simplify the work of the agency by helping to organize the relevant facts and to identify the controlling issues. What is the reason for denying the veteran the right to counsel of his choice in such cases? The Court gives us two answers: First, the paternalistic interest in protecting the veteran from the consequences of his own improvidence; and second, the bureaucratic interest in minimizing the cost of administering the benefit program. I agree that both interests are legitimate, but neither provides an adequate justification for the restraint on liberty imposed by the $10-fee limitation. . . .

In my opinion, the bureaucratic interest in minimizing the cost of administration is nothing but a red herring. Congress has not prohibited lawyers from participating in the processing of claims for benefits and there is no reason why it should. The complexity of the agency procedures can be regulated by limiting the number of hearings, the time for argument, the length of written submissions, and in other ways, but there is no reason to believe that the *agency's* cost of administration will be increased because a claimant is represented by counsel instead of appearing *pro se*. . . .

The paternalistic interest in protecting the veteran from his own improvidence would unquestionably justify a rule that simply prevented lawyers from over-charging their clients. Most appropriately, such a rule might require agency approval, or perhaps judicial review, of counsel fees. It might also establish a reasonable ceiling, subject to exceptions for especially complicated cases. In fact, I assume that the . . . limitation was justified by this interest when it was first enacted in 1864. But time has brought changes in the value of the dollar, in the character of the legal profession, in agency procedures, and in the ability of the veteran to proceed without the assistance of counsel. . . .

The fundamental error in the Court's analysis is its assumption that the individual's right to employ counsel of his choice in a contest with his sovereign is a kind of second-class interest that can be assigned a material value

and balanced on a utilitarian scale of costs and benefits. It
is true that the veteran's right to benefits is a property
right and that in fashioning the procedures for administering the benefit program, the Government may appropriately weigh the value of additional procedural safeguards against their precuniary costs. . . . But we are not
considering a procedural right that would involve any cost
to the Government. . . .

In my view, regardless of the nature of the dispute between the sovereign and the citizen—whether it be a criminal trial, a proceeding to terminate parental rights, a
claim for social security benefits, a dispute over welfare
benefits, or a pension claim asserted by the widow of a sol-
dier who was killed on the battlefield—the citizen's right
to consult an independent lawyer and to retain the lawyer
to speak on his or her behalf is an aspect of liberty that is
priceless. It should not be bargained away on the notion
that a totalitarian appraisal of the mass of claims pro-
cessed by the Veterans' Administration does not identify
an especially high probability of error.

Unfortunately, the reason for the Court's mistake today
is all too obvious. It does not appreciate the value of individual liberty.

Last, a dissent from the Court's ruling that the Constitution
does not bar police from telling a lawyer that a client in their
custody would not be interrogated that day, then proceeding to
interrogate, saying nothing of the lawyer's phone call. *Moran v.
Burbine,* 106 S.Ct. 1135, 1160, 1161–62 (1986). How *not* to balance.

. . . [S]ettled principles about construing waivers of constitutional rights and about the need for strict presump-
tions in custodial interrogations, as well as a plain reading
of the Miranda opinion itself, overwhelmingly support the
conclusion reached by almost every state court that has
considered the matter—a suspect's waiver of his right to
counsel is invalid if police refuse to inform the suspect of
his counsel's communications.

The Court makes the alternative argument that requiring police to inform a suspect of his attorney's communica-

tions to and about him is not required because it would upset the careful "balance" of Miranda. Despite its earlier notion that the attorney's call is an "outside event" that has "no bearing" on a knowing and intelligent waiver, the majority does acknowledge that information of attorney Munson's call "would have been useful to respondent" and "might have affected his decision to confess." Thus, a rule requiring the police to inform a suspect of an attorney's call would have two predictable effects. It would serve "Miranda's goal of dispelling the compulsion inherent in custodial interrogation," and it would disserve the goal of custodial interrogation because it would result in fewer confessions. By a process of balancing these two concerns, the Court finds the benefit to the individual outweighed by the "substantial cost to society's legitimate and substantial interest in securing admissions of guilt."

The Court's balancing approach is profoundly misguided. The cost of suppressing evidence of guilt will always make the value of a procedural safeguard appear "minimal," "marginal," or "incremental." Indeed, the value of any trial at all seems like a "procedural technicality" when balanced against the interest in administering prompt justice to a murderer or rapist caught redhanded. The individual interest in procedural safeguards that minimize the risk of error is easily discounted when the fact of guilt appears certain beyond doubt.

What is the cost of requiring the police to inform a suspect of his attorney's call? It would decrease the likelihood that custodial interrogation will enable the police to obtain a confession. This is certainly a real cost, but it is the same cost that this Court has repeatedly found necessary to preserve the character of our free society and our rejection of an inquisitorial system. . . .

If the Court's cost benefit analysis were sound, it would justify a repudiation of the right to a warning about counsel itself. . . . In either case, the withholding of information serves precisely the same law enforcement interests. And in both cases, the cost can be described as nothing more than an incremental increase in the risk that an individual will make an unintelligent waiver of his rights.

In cases like Escobedo, Miranda, and Dunaway, the

Court has viewed the balance from a much broader perspective. In all these cases—indeed, whenever the distinction between an inquisitorial and an accusatorial system of justice is implicated—the law enforcement interest served by incommunicado interrogation has been weighed against the interest in individual liberty that is threatened by such practices. The balance has never been struck by an evaluation of empirical data of the kind submitted to legislative decisionmakers—indeed, the Court relies on no such data today. Rather, the Court has evaluated the quality of the conflicting rights and interests. In the past, that kind of balancing process has led to the conclusion that the police have *no right* to compel an individual to respond to custodial interrogation, and that the interest in liberty that is threatened by incommunicado interrogation is so precious that special procedures must be followed to protect it. The Court's contrary conclusion today can only be explained by its failure to appreciate the value of the liberty that an accusatorial system seeks to protect.

Notes

Preface

1. B. Cardozo, *The Nature of the Judicial Process* (1920); A. Bickel, *The Least Dangerous Branch* (1962).

2. United States v. Carolene Products Co., 304 U.S. 144 (1938); United States v. Darby Lumber Co., 312 U.S. 100 (1941).

3. Hodel v. Virginia Surface Mining & Reclamation Assn., 452 U.S. 264 (1981); Federal Energy Regulatory Commission v. Mississippi, 456 U.S. 742 (1982); Garcia v. San Antonio Metropolitan Transit Authority, 469 U.S. 528 (1985). Compare National League of Cities v. Usery, 426 U.S. 833, 880 (1976), dissenting opinion, commenting on the taxing and spending power as well as commerce; EEOC v. Wyoming, 460 U.S. 226, 244 (1983), concurring opinion. In 1987, to cite a more recent example, Stevens joined the majority in upholding the use of the spending power to induce states to set the drinking age at twenty-one, South Dakota v. Dole, 107 S.Ct. 2793 (1987).

4. Complete Auto Transit, Inc. v. Brady, 430 U.S. 274 (1977); National Geographic Society v. California Board of Equalization, 430 U.S. 551 (1977); Exxon Corp. v. Governor of Maryland, 437 U.S. 117 (1978); City of Philadelphia v. New Jersey, 437 U.S. 617 (1978); Kassel v. Consolidated Freightways Corp., 450 U.S. 662 (1981); Thornburgh v. American Coll. of Obst. & Gyn., 106 S.Ct. 2169, 2185 (1986), concurring opinion.

5. United States v. Curtiss-Wright Export Corp., 299 U.S. 304 (1936); Goldwater v. Carter, 444 U.S. 996 (1979); Dames & Moore v. Regan, 453 U.S. 654 (1981).

6. Immigration and Naturalization Service v. Chadha, 462 U.S. 919 (1983); Bowsher v. Synar, 106 S.Ct. 3181 (1986), Stevens concurring in the judgment at 3181.

7. R. E. Riggs and L. C. McCarrey, "Justice Stevens and the Law of Antitrust," 43 *U. Pitt. L. Rev.* 649, esp. 667, 668 (1982). See also P. M. Gerhart, "The Supreme Court and Antitrust Analysis: The (Near) Triumph of the Chicago School," 1982 *Sup. Ct. Rev.* 351–80; E. R. Johnston and J. P. Stevens, "Monopoly or Monopolization—A Reply to Professor Rostow," 44 *Ill. L. Rev.* 269–97 (1949), arguing that mere size is not unlawful.

Chapter 1

1. *New York Times,* Feb. 6, 1977, p. 24; *Wall Street Journal,* Jan. 26, 1978, p. 1; *Time,* July 21, 1980, p. 76. Compare Elder Witt, "Perspective," *Congressional Quarterly Weekly Report,* Jan. 1, 1984, at 166 (Stevens a "liberal"); U.S. Congress, Senate, Committee on the Judiciary, *Hearings on the Nomination of John Paul Stevens to be an Associate Justice of the Supreme Court of the United States,* 94th Cong., 1st sess., 1975, at 32–33 (Stevens rejects labels). He was still sufficiently unknown in 1977 to be called "Harold" Stevens in an *Atlantic* article: A. U. Schwartz, "Danger: Pendulum Swing," February 1977, p. 31. Even in 1987, an Associated Press telephone poll of 1,223 adults found that fewer people (15 percent) had an opinion of Stevens, favorable or unfavorable, than of any other member of the Supreme Court. The second most obscure was Byron White (19 percent); the third, Harry Blackmun (20 percent); the least obscure, Sandra Day O'Connor (38 percent). *Albuquerque Journal,* Sept. 14, 1987, p. A10. The main lesson seems to be that moderates are inconspicuous.

2. Groppi v. Leslie, 436 F.2d 331, 332 (1971), dissenting opinion. Primary reliance will be on concurring and dissenting opinions throughout as the most reliable reflection of Stevens's own views.

3. Ibid. at 332, 334, 336.

4. Ibid. at 335. Footnote numbers are omitted in all quotations, as are all but a few citations of cases within quotations.

5. United States v. Smith, 440 F.2d 521, 527 (1971), dissenting opinion.

6. Idem.

7. Idem.

8. Ibid. at 530–31.

9. Ibid. at 528, 535.

10. Ibid. at 529, 533.

11. Ibid. at 535, 527.

12. Groppi v. Leslie at 333 n. 3, quoting Joint Anti-Fascist Refugee Committee v. McGrath, 341 U.S. 123, 162–63 (1951); for a similar view, see P. A. Freund, "The Supreme Court and Civil Liberties," 4 *Vand. L. Rev.* 545 (1951).

13. Ibid. at 332, 336.

14. Jones & Laughlin Steel Corp. v. Pfeifer, 462 U.S. 523, 552 (1983).

15. United States v. Smith at 527, 534.

16. J. P. Stevens, "Mr. Justice Rutledge," in *Mr. Justice,* at 333 (A. Dunham and P. B. Kurland eds. [1956] 1964).

17. Miller v. School District, 495 F.2d 658, 667 (1974).

18. Ibid. at 668 n. 34; "Mr. Justice Rutledge" at 331.

19. United States v. Ross, 456 U.S. 798, 801–2 (1982).

20. Ibid. at 800.

21. Carroll v. United States, 267 U.S. 132 (1925).

22. United States v. Ross at 803, 804, 820–21.

23. Ibid. at 807 n. 9, 812 n. 16, 813 n. 18.

24. Morales v. Schmidt, 494 F.2d 85, 87 (1974), concurring opinion; W. James, *Pragmatism* 67, 68 (1907).

25. Hudson v. Palmer, 468 U.S. 517, 552–53, 553 n. 29 (1984).

26. Snepp v. United States, 444 U.S. 507, 516–17 (1980), dissenting opinion.

27. Ibid. at 526.

28. Pennsylvania v. Mimms, 434 U.S. 106, 117 (1977), dissenting opinion.

29. Ibid. at 120–21.

30. Globe Newspaper Co. v. Superior Court, 457 U.S. 596, 620–21 (1982), dissenting opinion; New York v. Ferber, 458 U.S. 747, 780–81 (1982), concurring in the judgment. See also Procunier v. Navarette, 434 U.S. 555, 569 (1978), dissenting opinion; Leis v. Flynt, 439 U.S. 438, 457–58 (1979), dissenting opinion; Jago v. Van Curen, 454 U.S. 14, 23, 26 (1981), dissenting opinion; Illinois v. Batchelder, 463 U.S. 1112, 1119–20 (1983), dissenting opinion; Florida v. Meyers, 466 U.S. 380, 383–87 (1984), dissenting opinion; California v. Chemehuevi Indian Tribe, 106 S. Ct. 289, 291–92 (1985), dissenting opinion; Delaware v. Fensterer, 106 S.Ct. 292, 296–97 (1985), concurring in the judgment.

31. Nixon v. Administrator of General Services, 433 U.S. 425, 472 (1977).

32. Ibid. at 486, concurring opinion.

33. Adamo Wrecking Co. v. United States, 434 U.S. 275, 294, 293 (1978), dissenting opinion. See also Industrial Union v. American Petroleum Institute, 448 U.S. 607, 611 (1980), plurality opinion (similar treatment of exposure to benzine).

34. Hoellen v. Annunzio, 468 F.2d 522 (1972).

35. Brewer v. Williams, 430 U.S. 387, 415 (1977), concurring opinion.

36. H & H Tire Co. v. United States Department of Transportation, 471 F.2d 350, 355 (1972).

37. Ibid. at 356–57, concurring opinion.

38. Christman v. Hanrahan, 500 F.2d 65, 67 (1974); 500 F.2d 701, 713 (1973).

39. Miller v. School District at 663.

40. Ibid. at 664.

41. Idem.

42. *Hearings* at 59.

43. "Mr. Justice Rutledge" at 324.

44. *Pragmatism* at 54–55.

45. United States v. Smith at 528.

46. United States v. Davis, 437 F.2d 928, 933 (1971); Lakeside v. Oregon, 435 U.S. 333, 345 (1978), dissenting opinion. See Chapter 3 for a fuller consideration of Lakeside v. Oregon.

47. Parker v. Randolph, 442 U.S. 62, 89 n. 10, 90 n. 12 (1979), dissenting opinion; see also Baldwin v. Alabama, 472 U.S. 372, 393 (1985), dissenting opinion; Richardson v. Marsh, 107 S.Ct. 1702, 1710 n. 1 (1987), dissenting opinion.

48. Rhode Island v. Innis, 446 U.S. 291, 307–8 (1980), dissenting opinion.

49. Ibid. at 311.

50. Ibid. at 314–15.

51. Ibid. at 315 n. 15. See also Arizona v. Mauro, 107 S.Ct. 1931, 1937 (1987), dissenting opinion.

52. In re Chase, 468 F.2d 128, 137 (1972), dissenting opinion.

53. Ibid. at 140.

54. Ibid. at 138, 138 n. 6.

55. Compare *Hearings* at 68.

56. Board of Education v. McCluskey, 458 U.S. 966, 972–73 (1982), dissenting opinion.

57. Ibid. at 971. See also Connecticut v. Barrett, 107 S.Ct. 828, 836 (1987), dissenting opinion.

58. Kissinger v. Reporters Committee, 445 U.S. 136, 161–62 (1980), concurring in part, dissenting in part.

59. United States v. Leon, 468 U.S. 897, 962 (1984).

60. Florida Department of Health v. Florida Nursing Home Assn., 450 U.S. 147, 153–55 (1981), concurring opinion. See also California v. Sierra Club, 451 U.S. 287, 300–301 (1981), concurring opinion.

61. Runyon v. McCrary, 427 U.S. 160, 191 (1976), concurring opinion; Jones v. Alfred H. Mayer Co., 392 U.S. 409 (1968).

62. Johnson v. Transportation Agency, Santa Clara, 107 S.Ct. 1442, 1458–59 (1987), concurring opinion; EEOC v. Wyoming, 460 U.S. 226, 249–50 (1983), concurring opinion. See also Wainwright v. Sykes, 433 U.S. 72, 94 (1977), concurring opinion; Dougherty County Bd. of Ed. v. White, 439 U.S. 32, 47 (1978), concurring opinion. In Atascadero State Hospital v. Scanlon, 473 U.S. 234, 304 (1985), he explains why he followed an incorrectly decided precedent and later changed his mind.

63. Ganz v. Bensinger, 480 F.2d 88, 89 (1973).

64. Rose v. Mitchell, 443 U.S. 545, 594 (1979), dissenting in part.

65. Hoellen v. Annunzio at 527.

66. Nebraska Press Assn. v. Stuart, 427 U.S. 539, 617 (1976), concurring in the judgment.

67. *New York Times,* August 5, 1984, pp. 1, 17; New Jersey v. T.L.O., 469 U.S. 325, 370 (1985), concurring in part, dissenting in part; Oregon v. Elstad, 470 U.S. 298, 364 (1985), dissenting opinion. Stevens's opinions in two early affirmative action cases are illustrative: Regents of University of California v. Bakke, 438 U.S. 265, 412 (1978), concurring in the judgment in part and dissenting in part (statutory rather than constitutional interpretation); Wygant v. Jackson Board of Education, 106 S.Ct. 1842, 1867 (1986), dissenting opinion (particularization).

68. Miller v. School District at 668 n. 35, quoting Hugo Black in Karr v. Schmidt, 401 U.S. 1201, 1203 (1971).

69. Ibid. at 667 n. 33.

70. Fedorenko v. United States, 449 U.S. 490, 530, 538 (1981), dissenting opinion.

71. Dalia v. United States, 441 U.S. 238, 263–64 (1979), dissenting opinion.

72. United States ex rel. Kirby v. Sturges, 510 F.2d 397, 408–9 (1975). See also Manson v. Brathwaite, 432 U.S. 98, 118 (1977), concurring in the judgment.

73. Briscoe v. LaHue, 460 U.S. 325, 339–40, 340 n. 23 (1983).

74. See HCSC-Laundry v. United States, 450 U.S. 1, 8 (1981), dissenting opinion; McElroy v. United States, 455 U.S. 642, 659 (1982), dissenting opinion; Director, OWCP v. Perini North River Assn., 459 U.S. 297, 325 (1983), dissenting opinion; Garcia v. United States, 469 U.S. 70, 80 (1984), dissenting opinion; "Mr. Justice Rutledge" at 326.

75. In Smith v. United States, 431 U.S. 291, 311 n. 1 (1977), dissenting opinion, Stevens notes that the statute in question was passed after less than an hour of congressional debate, without objection in either house.

76. Delaware Tribal Business Committee v. Weeks, 430 U.S. 73, 96, 94, 98 (1977), dissenting opinion; also see Illinois State Board of Elections v. Socialist Workers Party, 440 U.S. 173, 189–90 (1979).

77. Fullilove v. Klutznick, 448 U.S. 448, 549–50 (1980), dissenting opinion.

78. Ibid. at 538–39, 542.

79. Bowen v. American Hospital Association, 106 S.Ct. 2113 (1986), plurality opinion; Adamo Wrecking Co. v. United States at 301 (quoting Earl Warren quoting Fred Vinson), 302.

80. In the matter of admission of Michael T. Rose, 71 L.Ed.2d 862 (1982), concurring opinion; with respect to juries, representing the conscience of the community, see Spaziano v. Florida, 468 U.S. 447, 486–89 (1984), concurring in part, dissenting in part.

81. Watt v. Alaska, 451 U.S. 259, 275 (1981), concurring opinion. See

also Watt v. Western Nuclear, Inc., 462 U.S. 36, 72 (1983), dissenting opinion; United States v. Young, 470 U.S. 1, 35 (1985), dissenting opinion.

82. Fitzgerald v. Porter Memorial Hospital, 523 F.2d 716, 721 (1975). See also Planned Parenthood of Central Missouri v. Danforth, 428 U.S. 52, 104–5 (1976), concurring in part, dissenting in part.

83. *Hearings* at 54.

84. K. Harmon et al., "The One Hundred and First Justice: An Analysis of the Opinions of Justice John Paul Stevens, Sitting as a Judge on the Seventh Circuit Court of Appeals," 29 *Vand. L. Rev.* 125 (1976), a well-researched student note that reaches conclusions about his appellate judging largely consistent with mine covering his work on both courts.

85. D. D. Eisenhower, *Mandate for Change* 230 (1963).

86. *Who's Who in America* (1986–87); *Chicago Tribune,* Nov. 11, 1975, p. 5.

87. *Daily Maroon,* April 18, 1940, p. 4. The full text is:

Tomorrow at noon a belligerent minority of the campus is going to parade in a peace demonstration. Supposedly representing the entire student body, the strikers will have two noble ends in view. First they want to show the country that the University of Chicago undergraduates are strongly for peace and against war; second they want to stimulate intelligent thinking on the subject of the best means of preserving American peace.

The ends are certainly desirable, but the means of striking for peace is unsatisfactory. The idea of putting on a big demonstration to show that Chicago students want peace is unnecessary to say the least. It must be obvious to any normal observer that these students do not want to participate in a war. The question that is debatable, however, is just when would they go to war? Would they be willing to fight if the country were invaded, if the Allies were losing or if an Allied victory seemed certain? A general, unorganized peace strike does not begin to answer the important question. The best way for the campus to express a definite opinion on the subject is to have a poll of the opinion of the entire student body. Such a poll would give an accurate expression of a major part of the campus, whereas the peace strike will give a vague expression of anti-war sentiment.

The second end, that of stimulating intelligent thinking on the subject of peace, cannot best be achieved by a strike. A strike undoubtedly induces some thinking on the subject, but it is hardly necessary to use artificial means of creating such thought when the whole country is following the hour by hour developments of the European conflict. The thing that is necessary is to provide for the constructive interchange of thought. Discussion designed to include opposed elements of the campus would be of great value in improving student thinking. The same can be said for any educational meeting, which may be held in conjunction with the peace demonstration, that tolerantly considers ways and means of preserving peace.

A peace strike is therefore inadequate because it fails to express an accurate student opinion, and is not in itself a sufficient stimulus to intelligent thinking on the subject. Nevertheless, the strike will go off on schedule, so that the world may learn something the world already knows.

88. *Who's Who in America* (1986–87); *Chicago Tribune,* Nov. 11, 1975, p. 5.

89. J. Corsi, *Judicial Politics* 138–39 (1984).

90. Letter to the author dated August 26, 1987.

91. *Chicago Tribune,* Nov. 11, 1975, p. 5; *New York Times,* Nov. 29, 1975, p. 1; *Hearings* at 4.

92. *Chicago Tribune,* Dec. 1, 1975, sec. 2, p. 2.

93. Letter to the author, above.

94. United States v. Butler, 297 U.S. 1, 62 (1936).

95. *Who Was Who in America,* 1982–85; Ashwander v. TVA, 297 U.S. 288, 341 (1936), concurring opinion.

96. Lochner v. New York, 198 U.S. 45, 76 (1905), dissenting opinion; J. P. Stevens, "Some Thoughts About a General Rule," 21 *Ariz. L. Rev.* 599, 604 n. 25 (1979).

97. L. Green, *Judge and Jury* 51–53 (1930); "Illinois Negligence Law," 39 *Ill. L. Rev.* 43 (1944).

98. L. Green, "My Philosophy of Law," in W. B. Kennedy et al., eds., *My Philosophy of Law* 134, 136 (1941); *Judge and Jury* at 269–76.

99. L. Green, "Unpacking the Court," *New Republic,* Feb. 24, 1937, pp. 67–68.

100. S. A. Baker, "John Paul Stevens," in L. Levy et al., eds., *Encyclopedia of the American Constitution* IV, 1764 (1986); J. P. Stevens, "Judicial Restraint," 22 *San Diego L. Rev.* 437, 441, 441 n. 10 (1985); C. A. Auerbach, "Tribute" [to Nathaniel Nathanson], 22 *San Diego L. Rev.* 431, 432 (1985).

101. F. A. Allen, *Law, Intellect, and Education* 17–21 (1979).

102. "Mr. Justice Rutledge" at 331, 332, 333, 329, 334.

103. Ibid. at 330, 334.

104. Ibid. at 324.

105. Ibid. at 329, 331, 333.

106. Ibid. at 331, 327–28.

107. Ibid. at 320–21, 324, 335, 340–41.

108. Ibid. at 324–25, 326, 329–30.

Chapter 2

1. See K. Karst, "Legislative Facts in Constitutional Litigation," 1960 *Sup. Ct. Rev.* 75, 78–79.

2. "Ad hoc" balancing is sometimes used as a general term embracing what I have called compound, case-by-case, and ad hoc. See, for example, M. Shapiro, *Freedom of Speech* 90–91 (1966); T. A. Aleinikoff, "Constitutional Law in the Age of Balancing," 96 *Yale L. J.* 943, 948 (1987).

3. Committee for Public Education v. Regan, 444 U.S. 646, 653 (1980).

4. Everson v. Board of Education, 330 U.S. 1, 16, 33 (1947).

5. Reynolds v. United States, 98 U.S. 145, 164 (1878).

6. Wolman v. Walter, 433 U.S. 229, 266 (1977), concurring in part and dissenting in part; Committee for Public Education v. Regan at 671, dissenting opinion.

7. Committee for Public Education v. Regan at 671.

8. Idem; Roemer v. Board of Public Works of Maryland, 426 U.S. 736, 775 (1976), dissenting opinion.

9. Buford v. Southeast Dubois County School Corp., 472 F.2d 890, 891–92 (1973). Stevens also participates in drawing lines between state activities affecting church schools which do and do not constitute establishment. Sometimes the Court rejects establishment claims unanimously, e.g., Witters v. Washington Department of Services for the Blind, 106 S.Ct. 748 (1986). In one case in which the Court was badly split, a majority found most of a bundle of state programs affecting church schools acceptable, Stevens found a few acceptable, and Brennan, even more clearly on the side of Jefferson, approved of none. Wolman v. Walter at 255–56, 264–66.

10. Roth v. United States, Alberts v. California, 354 U.S. 476, 481 (1957).

11. Chaplinsky v. New Hampshire, 315 U.S. 568, 571–72 (1942).

12. Roth v. United States at 484, 488–89.

13. Quoted in H. Kalven, "The Metaphysics of the Law of Obscenity," 1960 *Sup. Ct. Rev.* 1, 44.

14. Jacobellis v. Ohio, 378 U.S. 184, 197 (1964).

15. Memoirs v. Massachusetts, 383 U.S. 413, 418 (1966).

16. Miller v. California, 413 U.S. 15, 24, 31–34 (1973).

17. Liles v. Oregon, 425 U.S. 963, 964 (1976), concurring opinion.

18. Ibid. at 963 n. 1.

19. Ibid. at 965–66, 964.

20. Marks v. United States, 430 U.S. 188, 198, 198 n. (1977), concurring in part, dissenting in part.

21. Smith v. United States, 431 U.S. 291, 311, 312 (1977), dissenting opinion.

22. Ibid. at 313–14, 315.

23. Ibid. at 314–15, 316.

24. Ward v. Illinois, 431 U.S. 767, 782 (1977), dissenting opinion.

25. Smith v. United States at 311.

26. Ibid. at 313. See also Pope v. Illinois, 107 S.Ct. 1918, 1927–30 (1987), dissenting opinion.

27. Smith v. United States at 317.

28. New York v. Ferber, 458 U.S. 747, 777–78 (1982), concurring in the judgment. Stevens recognized another exception in 1987: ". . . government may not constitutionally criminalize mere possession or sale of obscene literature, absent some connection to minors, *or obtrusive display to unconsenting adults.*" Pope v. Illinois at 1927 (emphasis added).

29. New York v. Ferber at 779.

30. U.S. Congress, Senate, Committee on the Judiciary, *Hearings on the Nomination of John Paul Stevens to be an Associate Justice of the Supreme Court of the United States,* 94th Cong., 1st sess., 1975, at 72–73.

31. Ibid. at 46, 59.

32. New York v. Ferber at 781; Schad v. Mt. Ephraim, 452 U.S. 61, 80 (1981), concurring in the judgment.

33. Young v. American Mini Theatres, Inc., 427 U.S. 50, 61 (1976).

34. Ibid. at 70–71.

35. Ibid. at 71.

36. See Schad v. Mt. Ephraim at 79; New York State Liquor Authority v. Bellanca, 452 U.S. 714, 718 (1981), dissenting opinion.

37. FCC v. Pacifica Foundation, 438 U.S. 726, 746 (1978).

38. Ibid. at 746–47.

39. Ibid. at 750–51.

40. Virginia State Board of Pharmacy v. Virginia Citizens Consumer Council, 425 U.S. 748 (1976).

41. Central Hudson Gas & Electric v. Public Service Commission, 447 U.S. 557, 579–80 (1980), Stevens concurring in the judgment.

42. Ibid. at 580; ibid. at 573–79, Blackmun concurring in the judgment; in Bolger v. Youngs Drug Products Corp., 463 U.S. 60, 81 (1983), Stevens, concurring in part, cautions against viewing commercial speech as a well-defined category.

43. Ibid. at 83.

44. Cary v. Population Services International, 431 U.S. 678, 712 (1977), concurring in part and concurring in the judgment; Metromedia, Inc. v. San Diego, 453 U.S. 490, 540 (1981), dissenting in part.

45. Carey v. Population Services International at 716–17.

46. Metromedia, Inc. v. San Diego at 552. For compound balancing in a case of libel of a private citizen, which fits more or less into the category of low-value speech, see Philadelphia Newspapers, Inc. v. Hepps, 106 S.Ct. 1558, 1566 (1986), dissenting opinion.

47. Metromedia, Inc. v. San Diego at 554–55.

48. *Hearings* at 47.

49. Brown v. Glines, 444 U.S. 348, 378–79 (1980), dissenting opinion.

50. Morales v. Schmidt, 489 F.2d 1335, 1346, 1346 n. 8 (1973).

51. Houchins v. KQED, Inc., 438 U.S. 1, 30 (1978), dissenting opinion.

52. Ibid. at 31 n. 21.

53. Ibid. at 31–32.

54. Ibid. at 32.

55. Ibid. at 32 n. 22.

56. Richmond Newspapers, Inc. v. Virginia, 448 U.S. 555, 582 (1980), concurring opinion.

57. Ibid. at 598, 601.

58. J. P. Stevens, "Some Thoughts About a General Rule," 21 *Ariz. L. Rev.* 599, 602 (1979); Nebraska Press Assn. v. Stuart, 427 U.S. 539, 617 (1976), concurring in the judgment.

59. Illinois State Employees Union v. Lewis, 473 F.2d 561 (1972). Because one of the other judges concurred separately and the third dissented, Judge Stevens's opinion of the court may fairly be taken as an expression of personal views. Branti v. Finkel, 445 U.S. 507 (1980).

60. Elrod v. Burns, 427 U.S. 347, 376–77 (1976).

61. Illinois State Employees Union v. Lewis at 570.

62. Ibid. at 576, 575. Compare FCC v. League of Women Voters, 468 U.S. 364, 408 (1984), dissenting opinion.

63. Consolidated Edison Co. v. Public Service Commission, 447 U.S. 530, 536 (1980).

64. Ibid. at 544–45, concurring in the judgment. See also NLRB v. Retail Store Employees, 447 U.S. 607, 618 (1980), concurring in part and concurring in the result. Compare his Senate testimony at n. 30, above.

65. Consolidated Edison Co. v. Public Service Commission at 545–46. See also Regan v.Time, Inc., 468 U.S. 641, 692 (1984), concurring in the judgment in part, dissenting in part; City Council v. Taxpayers for Vincent, 466 U.S. 789, 814–15 (1984); Cornelius v. NAACP, 473 U.S. 788, 833–36 (1985), dissenting opinion; Bolger v. Youngs Drug Products Corp. at 84. See also Arkansas Writers' Project, Inc. v. Ragland, 107 S.Ct. 1722, 1730 (1987), concurring in part and concurring in the judgment.

66. After J. H. Ely, *Democracy and Distrust* 110 (1980); also see L. H. Tribe, *Constitutional Choices* 396–97 n. 61 (1985). On occasion the Court strikes down regulation by subject matter, e.g., Police Department of Chicago v. Mosley, 408 U.S. 92 (1972).

67. Widmar v. Vincent, 454 U.S. 263, 278 (1981), concurring in the judgment.

68. Ibid. at 267–68, 277.

69. Ibid. at 277, 278.

70. Ibid. at 280–81.

71. Consolidated Edison Co. v. Public Service Commission at 546; Widmar v. Vincent at 279 n. 2.

Chapter 3

1. Groppi v. Leslie, 436 F.2d 331, 332 (1971), dissenting opinion.

2. United States v. Smith, 440 F.2d 521, 527 (1971), dissenting opinion.

3. United States v. Thomas, 463 F.2d 1061, 1063, 1064 (1972), dissenting opinion.

4. Ibid. at 1065, 1065 n. 2.

5. Ibid. at 1065–66.

6. Idem.

7. United States v. Hasting, 461 U.S. 499, 517 (1983), concurring in the judgment.

8. Rogers v. Loether, 467 F.2d 1110, 1111–12 (1972).

9. United States v. Lovasco, 431 U.S. 783, 798 n. 2, 799 (1977), dissenting opinion. See also Nixon v. Warner Communications, Inc., 435 U.S. 589, 613–15 (1978), dissenting opinion.

10. Fed. Rules Civ. Proc. 52(a); Denison Mines, Ltd. v. Michigan Chemical Corp., 469 F.2d 1301, 1310 (1972).

11. Douglas Oil Co. v. Petrol Stops Northwest, 441 U.S. 211, 236–37 (1979), dissenting opinion.

12. Bachner v. United States, 517 F.2d 589, 599 (1975), concurring opinion; Rushen v. Spain, 464 U.S. 114, 128 (1983), concurring in the judgment.

13. United States v. Trutenko, 490 F.2d 678, 679 (1973). Since one of the other two judges dissented, Stevens's opinion of the court may be assumed to be a reasonably fair reflection of personal views.

14. Ibid. at 681, 679; Kotteakos v. United States, 328 U.S. 750, 764 (1946).

15. Nixon v. Warner Communications, Inc. at 613–16.

16. United States v. Greene, 497 F.2d 1068, 1087–88 (1974), dissenting opinion.

17. Ibid. at 1090, 1091, 1092.

18. Lakeside v. Oregon, 435 U.S. 333, 334, 334 n. 2, 335 (1978).

19. Ibid. at 340.

20. Ibid. at 345, 346 n. 6, dissenting opinion.

21. Ibid. at 347–48.

22. United States v. Barrett, 505 F.2d 1091, 1107–8 (1974), dissenting opinion.

23. Ibid. at 1115.

24. United States v. Ott, 489 F.2d 872, 873 (1973).

25. Ibid. at 873–74, 875 n. 8, 875.

26. Bell v. Burson, 402 U.S. 535, 540 (1971).

27. Morrissey v. Brewer, 408 U.S. 471, 481 (1972).

28. Board of Regents v. Roth, 408 U.S. 564, 570–71, 579 (1972).

29. Shirck v. Thomas, 447 F.2d 1025, 1028, (1971), dissenting opinion;

Thomas v. Shirck, 408 U.S. 940 (1972); Shirck v. Thomas, 486 F.2d 691, 692 (1973).

30. Board of Regents v. Roth at 571, 572–73, 575.

31. Ibid. at 576, 577.

32. Jeffries v. Turkey Run Consolidated School District, 492 F.2d 1, 3–4 (1974).

33. Bishop v. Wood, 426 U.S. 341, 347–48, 350 (1976).

34. Kimbrough v. O'Neil, 523 F.2d 1057, 1064 (1975), concurring opinion; Shirck v. Thomas (1971) at 1029.

35. Idem.

36. Jeffries v. Turkey Run Consolidated School District at 4; Kimbrough v. O'Neil at 1064.

37. Kimbrough v. O'Neil at 1063.

38. Jeffries v. Turkey Run Consolidated School District at 4 n. 12.

39. Ibid. at 4 n. 8; Kimbrough v. O'Neil at 1066.

40. Bishop v. Wood at 349–50.

41. 42 U.S.C. sec. 1983, from Act of April 20, 1871, c. 22, sec. 1, 17 Stat. 13.

42. Kimbrough v. O'Neil at 1063.

43. Florida v. Meyers, 466 U.S. 380, 385 (1984), dissenting opinion.

44. Kimbrough v. O'Neil at 1064.

45. United States ex rel. Miller v. Twomey, 479 F.2d 701, 713 (1973). Stevens's opinion of the court may be taken as his personal position: see Meachum v. Fano, 427 U.S. 215, 232 (1976).

46. Bell v. Wolfish, 441 U.S. 520 (1979).

47. Ibid. at 583, 584, 586, dissenting opinion.

48. Ibid. at 592, 593.

49. Ibid. at 593–95.

50. Miller v. School District, 495 F.2d 658, 663, 664 (1974).

51. Fitzgerald v. Porter Memorial Hospital, 523 F.2d 716, 721 (1975).

52. United States ex rel. Miller v. Twomey at 712, 713, 717.

53. Ibid. at 717–18.

54. Ibid. at 716.

55. Lassiter v. Department of Social Services, 452 U.S. 18, 59–60 (1981), dissenting opinion; also Walters v. Nat. Assn. of Radiation Survivors, 473 U.S. 305, 371 (1985), dissenting opinion (see Appendix).

56. Board of Regents v. Roth at 577.

57. Adams v. Walker, 492 F.2d 1003, 1009 (1974), concurring opinion.

58. Bishop v. Wood at 344.

59. Meachum v. Fano at 230, dissenting opinion.

60. Ibid. at 233. See also Hudson v. Palmer, 468 U.S. 517, 542, 547–48 (1984), concurring in part, dissenting in part.

61. Kimbrough v. O'Neil at 1065.

62. Ingraham v. Wright, 430 U.S. 651, 701 (1977), dissenting opinion.

63. Moore v. East Cleveland, 431 U.S. 494, 520 (1977), concurring in the judgment.

64. United States v. Shaheen, 445 F.2d 6, 10 (1971).

65. Vance v. Terrazas, 444 U.S. 252, 274 (1980), concurring in part, dissenting in part.

66. J. P. Stevens, "Mr. Justice Rutledge," in *Mr. Justice,* at 329 (A. Dunham and P. B. Kurland eds. [1956] 1964).

67. J. N. Frank, "Words and Music," 47 *Colum. L. Rev.* 1259–78 (1947).

Chapter 4

1. Korematsu v. United States, 323 U.S. 214, 216 (1944).

2. Craig v. Boren, 429 U.S. 190, 197 (1976).

3. E.g., McGowan v. Maryland, 366 U.S. 420, 425–26 (1961).

4. Craig v. Boren at 211–12, concurring opinion. See also Cleburne v. Cleburne Living Center, 105 S.Ct. 3249, 3260–63 (1985), concurring opinion; Cornelius v. NAACP Legal Defense and Ed. Fund, 473 U.S. 788, 833 (1985), dissenting opinion. For comparable criticism of the majority view by Justice Marshall, see San Antonio Independent School District v. Rodriguez, 411 U.S. 1, 98–100 (1973).

5. General Electric Co. v. Gilbert, 429 U.S. 125, 133, 134–35 (1976); Geduldig v. Aiello, 417 U.S. 484, 496 n. 20 (1974).

6. General Electric Co. v. Gilbert at 136, 138.

7. Ibid. at 161–62, 161 n. 5, dissenting opinion. As Stevens notes in his opinion of the Court in Newport News Shipbuilding & Dry Dock v. EEOC, 462 U.S. 669, 670 (1983), Congress amended Title VII in 1978 to prohibit sex discrimination on the basis of pregnancy.

8. Nashville Gas Co. v. Satty, 434 U.S. 136, 153–54 (1977), concurring in the judgment.

9. Ibid. at 155.

10. Los Angeles Dept. of Water & Power v. Manhart, 435 U.S. 702 (1978).

11. Ibid. at 715.

12. Ibid at 725, 725 n.

13. Sprogis v. United Air Lines, Inc., 444 F.2d 1194, 1205 (1971), dissenting opinion.

14. Idem.

15. U.S. Congress, Senate, Committee on the Judiciary, *Hearings on the Nomination of John Paul Stevens to be an Associate Justice of the Supreme Court of the United States,* 94th Cong., 1st sess., 1975, at 227, 226, 79, 83.

16. Ibid. at 15.

17. United Air Lines, Inc. v. Evans, 431 U.S. 553, 557–58 (1977).

18. Wengler v. Druggists Mutual Insurance Co., 446 U.S. 142, 154–55 (1980), concurring in the judgment.

19. Personnel Administrator of Massachusetts v. Feeney, 442 U.S. 256, 281 (1979), concurring opinion.

20. Cousins v. City Council, 466 F.2d 830, 850, 852, 853 (1972), dissenting opinion (emphasis added by Justice Stevens).

21. Mobile v. Bolden, 446 U.S. 55, 86 (1980), concurring in the judgment.

22. Cousins v. City Council at 856, 856 n. 32. Occasionally the theme appears in other kinds of cases, e.g., Dayton Board of Education v. Brinkman, 433 U.S. 406, 421 (1977), school desegregation; Hoellen v. Annunzio, 468 F.2d 522, 526 (1972), the franking privilege; Estelle v. Gamble, 429 U.S. 97, 116 (1976), cruel and unusual punishment; Dunaway v. New York, 442 U.S. 200, 220 (1979), search and seizure.

23. Cousins v. City Council at 856–57.

24. Washington v. Davis, 426 U.S. 229, 253 (1976), concurring opinion.

25. Ibid. at 254.

26. Dayton Board of Education v. Brinkman at 421 (1977), concurring opinion.

27. Mobile v. Bolden at 90, 93.

28. Rogers v. Lodge, 458 U.S. 613, 642–43 (1982), dissenting opinion. See also Karcher v. Daggett, 462 U.S. 725, 753–54 (1983), concurring opinion.

29. Rose v. Bridgeport Brass Company, 487 F.2d 804, 812 (1973), dissenting in part.

30. Ibid. at 805–6.

31. Ibid. at 813.

32. Washington v. Davis at 237.

33. Ibid. at 254–55.

34. New York City Transit Authority v. Beazer, 440 U.S. 568, 573, 579 (1979).

35. Ibid. at 576, 577, 593 n. 40.

36. Caban v. Mohammed, 441 U.S. 380, 403 n. 6, 401 (1979), dissenting opinion.

37. Ibid. at 404–7.

38. Mathews v. Diaz, 426 U.S. 67, 79–80 (1976).

39. Ibid. at 80–82.

40. E.g., Mathews v. Lucas, 427 U.S. 495, 516 (1976), dissenting opinion, on illegitimacy.

41. Cousins v. City Council at 856.

42. Ibid. at 859.

43. Idem.

44. Ibid. at 847; Gomillion v. Lightfoot, 364 U.S. 339, 340, 341, 342 (1960).

45. Cousins v. City Council at 859–60.

46. Ibid. at 860.

47. Ibid. at 861; Cousins v. City Council, 503 F.2d 912, 925 (1974), concurring opinion.

48. Karcher v. Daggett at 762.

49. Washington v. Davis at 254; Mobile v. Bolden at 86. See also United States v. Paradise, 107 S.Ct. 1702, 1713 (1987), concurring in the judgment.

50. Yick Wo v. Hopkins, 118 U.S. 356, 373 (1886).

51. Mobile v. Bolden at 84, 83, 84, 86.

52. Ibid. at 91–92.

53. Ibid. at 92, 92 n. 14.

54. McGowan v. Maryland at 425–26.

55. Foley v. Connelie, 435 U.S. 291, 307–8 (1978), dissenting opinion.

56. Nickols v. Gagnon, 454 F.2d 467, 472 (1971).

57. Califano v. Jobst, 434 U.S. 47, 52–53 (1977).

58. New York City Transit Authority v. Beazer at 592–93.

59. Caban v. Mohammed at 411–12; City of Rome v. United States, 446 U.S. 156 (1980), concurring opinion; H. L. v. Matheson, 450 U.S. 398, 424–25 (1981), concurring in the judgment; Cooper v. Bernalillo County Assessor, 472 U.S. 612, 632–33 (1985), dissenting opinion.

60. Mathews v. Lucas at 515–16.

61. Ibid. at 518, 522–23.

62. Craig v. Boren at 212–13, 213 n. 4, 214.

63. Zablocki v. Redhail, 434 U.S. 374, 403 (1978), concurring in the judgment.

64. Craig v. Boren at 211.

65. Mathews v. Lucas at 520–21.

66. Craig v. Boren at 212.

Chapter 5

1. R. Dworkin, *Taking Rights Seriously* 190–96 (1978).

2. Ibid. at 191, 198. In a thoughtful, comprehensive analysis of balancing, T. A. Aleinikoff argues that indeed it need not serve illiberal interests, but he is critical on other grounds, among them that balancers pretend to be more scientific than they are. He cites Stevens as both a balancer and a critic of "scientific" balancing, but in the end omits his name from a list (Blackmun, Brennan, Marshall, Powell, and White) of those who "frequently adopt a balancing approach"! "Constitutional Law in the Age of Balancing," 96 *Yale L. J.* 943, 944, 993, 968 n. 160, 992 n. 273, 964–65 (1987).

3. Barenblatt v. United States, 360 U.S. 109, 126, 128, 134, 141, 142, 143 (1959). See C. R. Ducat, *Modes of Constitutional Interpretation* 156–65 (1978).

4. K. Karst, "Legislative Facts in Constitutional Litigation," 1960 *Sup. Ct. Rev.* 79–80; A. Meiklejohn, *Political Freedom* 39–42 (1960).

5. J. H. Ely, *Democracy and Distrust* (1980); United States v. Caro-lene Products Co., 304 U.S. 144, 152 n. 4 (1938).

6. *Democracy and Distrust* at 113 n., 109, 111–15; Brandenburg v. Ohio, 395 U.S. 444 (1969); Cohen v. California, 403 U.S. 15 (1971).

7. *Democracy and Distrust* at 107, 108, 116.

8. Barenblatt v. United States at 144, 145. Also see his dissent in Scales v. United States, 367 U.S. 203, 261 (1961), criticizing the "free-dom-destroying nature of the 'balancing test' presently in use by the Court to justify its refusal to apply specific constitutional protections of the Bill of Rights." Black is open to similar criticism for his opinion of the Court in Korematsu v. United States, 323 U.S. 214 (1944), the key Japanese exclusion case.

9. "Legislative Facts in Constitutional Litigation" at 84.

10. United States v. Leon, 468 U.S. 897 (1984); Massachusetts v. Shep-pard, 468 U.S. 981 (1984); F. H. Easterbrook, "The Supreme Court, 1983 Term—Forward: The Court and the Economic System," 98 *Harv. L. Rev.* 4 (1984); L. H. Tribe, "Constitutional Calculus: Equal Justice or Eco-nomic Efficiency?" 98 *Harv. L. Rev.* 592 (1984); F. H. Easterbrook, "Method, Result, and Authority: A Reply," 98 *Harv. L. Rev.* 596, 597 (1985).

11. United States v. Leon at 901–2.

12. Ibid. at 902–3.

13. Massachusetts v. Sheppard at 984–87.

14. United States v. Leon at 900–901.

15. Ibid. at 906–8, 909, 910, 916, 917, 922; Massachusetts v. Sheppard at 988–89.

16. R. Posner, *Economic Analysis of the Law* pt. VII (2d ed. 1977).

17. "The Supreme Court, 1983 Term" at 10, 12; *Economic Analysis of the Law* at 10, 11 (emphasis in original omitted).

18. "The Supreme Court, 1983 Term" at 59, 59 n. 157.

19. United States v. Leon at 931, 938–39, 940, 941, 942, 948, 955.

20. Ibid. at 946, 929, 930.

21. Ibid. at 942, 929, 943.

22. "Constitutional Calculus" at 607.

23. Ibid. at 609; United States v. Leon at 953–58, 974–76.

24. "Constitutional Calculus" at 597, 596; "Method, Result, and Au-thority" at 623; *Economic Analysis of the Law* at 21–22.

25. United States v. Leon at 960–80.

26. B. Cardozo, *The Nature of the Judicial Process,* 14, 18, 21, 28, 31, 43, 162, 113 (1920).

27. United States v. Leon at 960–66.

28. Ibid. at 974; 979 n. 38; 979, quoting Justice Jackson in Harris v. United States, 331 U.S. 145, 198 (1947).

29. "Constitutional Calculus" at 595, 607–14.

30. Ibid. at 599–606.

31. If Stevens writes a purely jurisdictional opinion, the case is omitted even though some or all other justices decide on the merits; a case in which two issues are taken up independently at some length is scored as two cases; but if the issues are intertwined (for example, the right to counsel and the right not to incriminate oneself in *Miranda* cases), each issue is scored as .5; an opinion concurring in part and dissenting in part is scored as a dissent. I have been guided, to the extent appropriate for this study, by the criteria set out in the annual November statistical analysis of Supreme Court voting in the *Harvard Law Review* and by D. W. Rohde and H. J. Spaeth, *Supreme Court Decision Making* 134–37 (1976). The percentages should be taken as approximate, since no two informed students of the Court could ever classify the dominant subject or subjects of each of hundreds of cases identically, regardless of the time and care devoted to the effort. Neither, however, would they be very far apart.

32. Florida v. Meyers, 466 U.S. 380, 386–87 (1984), dissenting opinion. Note that cases such as these are not included in the tabulations and charts in this chapter.

33. *New York Times,* Aug. 5, 1987, p. 1; Oct. 26, 1985, p. 1; October 28, 1985, p. A12.

34. For example, L. Pfeffer, *Religion, State and the Burger Court* xi–xiv (1984).

35. Pennsylvania v. Mimms, 434 U.S. 106, 123 n. 13 (1977), dissenting opinion; K. C. Davis, *Administrative Law Treatise* secs. 15.2, 15.3 (2d ed. 1980).

36. FCC v. Pacifica Foundation, 438 U.S. 726, 748, 749 n. 27, 749, 739, 750 n. 29, 749, 751, 750 (1978).

37. Roe v. Wade, 410 U.S. 113 (1973); FCC v. Pacifica Foundation at 734–35, 739, 742, 744, 750.

38. Castenada v. Partida, 430 U.S. 482, 483–97 (1977); Ballew v. Georgia, 435 U.S. 223, 231–39 (1978); Craig v. Boren, 429 U.S. 190, 213–14 (1976), concurring opinion; Karcher v. Daggett, 462 U.S. 725, 744 (1983), concurring opinion; Caban v. Mohammed, 441 U.S. 380, 401 (1979), dissenting opinion; Richardson v. Marsh, 107 S.Ct. 1702, 1713 (1987), dissenting opinion; California v. Carney, 471 U.S. 386, 399, 399 n. 9 (1985), dissenting opinion; Pennsylvania v. Mimms at 118–19, 121, dissenting opinion; H & H Tire Company v. United States Department of Transportation, 471 F.2d 350, 356–57 (1972); Goldman v. Weinberger, 106 S.Ct. 1310, 1316 (1986), concurring opinion. Compare Brown-Foreman v. N.Y. Liquor Authority, 106 S.Ct. 2080, 2088 (1986), dissenting opinion.

39. L. H. Tribe, *Constitutional Choices* 7–8 (1985).

40. For example, Moran v. Burbine, 106 S.Ct. 1135, 1160–62 (1986), dissenting opinion (see Appendix).

41. *Taking Rights Seriously* at 194.

42. United States ex rel. Miller v. Twomey, 479 F.2d 701, 713 (1973);

Meachum v. Fano, 427 U.S. 215, 233 (1976); Bell v. Wolfish, 441 U.S. 520, 592, 593 (1979); Morales v. Schmidt, 489 F2d 1335, 1346, 1346 n. 8 (1973); Houchins v. KQED, Inc., 438 U.S. 1, 30 (1978); Richmond Newspapers, Inc. v. Virginia, 448 U.S. 555, 582 (1980); Illinois State Employees Union v. Lewis, 473 F.2d 561 (1972); Branti v. Finkel, 445 U.S. 507 (1980); Roemer v. Board of Public Works of Maryland, 426 U.S. 736, 775 (1976).

43. *Constitutional Choices* at 7.

44. City Council v. Taxpayers for Vincent, 466 U.S. 789, 815 n. 32 (1984).

45. Dennis v. United States, 341 U.S. 494, 517 (1951), dissenting opinion.

46. G. Gunther, "In Search of Judicial Quality on a Changing Court," 24 *Stanf. L. Rev.* 1001, 1013–14 (1972).

47. Richmond Newspapers, Inc. v. Virginia, above; Fullilove v. Klutznick, 448 U.S. 448 (1980).

48. United States v. Leon, above.

49. New Jersey v. T.L.O., 469 U.S. 325, 340–41, 371, 377, 342 n. 9 (1985).

50. Thornburgh v. American Coll. of Obst. & Gyn., 106 S.Ct. 2169, 2196, 2188 (1986); Roe v. Wade, above.

51. Thornburgh v. American Coll. of Obst. & Gyn. at 2188, 2196–97.

52. Ibid. at 2194.

53. Ibid. at 2187 n. 5, 2189–90.

54. Ibid. at 2189 n. 10.

55. Ibid. at 2189 n. 10, 2194–95.

56. New Jersey v. T.L.O. at 351–53. See also United States v. Leon at 927–28; Goldman v. Weinberger at 1322–24 (1986).

57. Roe v. Wade, above.

58. *New York Times,* July 12, 1987, p. 9.

59. National League of Cities v. Usery, 426 U.S. 833 (1976); Garcia v. San Antonio Metropolitan Transit Authority, 469 U.S. 528 (1985); Regents of the University of California v. Bakke, 438 U.S. 265 (1978).

60. *New York Times,* July 12, 1987, p. 9.

Epilogue

1. H. J. Abraham, *Justices & Presidents* 65–66 (2d ed. 1985).

2. V. Blasi, "The Rootless Activism of the Burger Court," in *The Burger Court: The Counter-Revolution That Wasn't* at 210, 211, 212 (V. Blasi ed. 1983). Also see, in the same spirit: "As Stevens began his service as a justice, knowledgeable observers expected him to become a

leader of the Court by virtue of his powerful intellect and moderate instincts. That has not happened. Instead, Stevens has tended to develop highly original, sometimes idiosyncratic theories that fail to win the endorsement of his brethren. He is a formidable but unconventional legal thinker. With Stevens operating as he has at the center of the Court's divisions, the effect of his independence of mind often has been to fragment potential majorities and leave the state of the law indeterminate." Ibid., "Profiles of the Justices," no author given, at 252.

3. See C. E. Lindblom, "The Science of Muddling Through," 19 *Pub. Adm. Rev.* 79–99 (1959).

4. W. James, *Pragmatism* 60 (1907).

General Index

Index of Cases